success from within

Brendan Hackett

NATIONAL COACHING & TRAINING CENTRE
IONAD NÁISIÚNTA OILIÚNA AGUS TRAENÁLA

Published in 1998 by
National Coaching & Training Centre
University of Limerick
Limerick, Ireland
Tel: + 353 (0) 61 202895
Fax: + 353 (0) 61 338174
http: //www ul. ie/generalinfo/nctchome.html

ISBN: 1-902550-00-5

Production Director: Frank Greally
Developmental Editor: Declan O'Leary
Design and Layout: Temple of Design
Cover Design: Mary Guinan
Photography: Billy Stickland, INPHO; Ray McManus, Sportsfile
Printed by: Kilkenny People

Printed in Republic of Ireland

ACKNOWLEDGMENTS

A great many people play a part in the creation of a book. There are those who inspire the author, and I would like to acknowledge some of them – my sporting heroes, the sportspeople I have worked with and coached, and a host of friends and associates.

There are those who support you as you try to bring ideas to fruition. In that context, my wife, Claire, stands head and shoulders above everybody. There are also the staff who work with me, particularly my brother John.

There are the people you need to bounce ideas off. I have exchanged many ideas with my good friend Liam Moggan during the writing of this book.

In the production of a book many professionals contribute. I would like to thank Suzanne Lynch, Deirdre O'Neill, Mary Guinan, Richard Gallagher, John Greene, the staff at Sportsfile and Inpho, Ger Corbett, Dr Aidan Moran, and last but by no means least my close friend and publisher Frank Greally. Frank inspired me to write through *Irish Runner* magazine. His support has been priceless.

Books are expensive to produce, and it is a tremendous boost when people show faith in your effort. I am indebted to the National Coaching and Training Centre for publishing the book. I would like to thank Pat Duffy, Sheelagh Quinn and Declan O'Leary for their help and encouragement. I would also like to sincerely thank adidas (Irl) Ltd for their support, especially their marketing manager, Paul Moloney.

Finally, books take perseverance. To all those people who were encouraging along the way, I can finally say Thanks!

Brendan Hackett
August 1998

CREDITS

Quotations

Cover Photographs

Front: D.J Carey, Catherina McKiernan, Maurice Fitzgerald and Packie Bonner.
Back: Darren Clarke and Sarah Kelleher.

"Sports training and performance rides on a rushing wind, a roar of flames and a rumble of thunder. There is much to be gained from regularly breaking and diving into pools of silence. Silence has a creative value when used to think, reflect, recall past enjoyable experiences and to contemplate all we have to be thankful for. In silence we may define our aims and assess our progress towards achieving them, face problems and work out ways to solve them."

Anthony Stewart

FOREWORD

Success in Sports

Irish people value success in sport. Whether in the role of participant, coach or administrator, the Irish generally want to achieve. But what is success in sport? Certainly, winning is important. Irish sportsmen and sportswomen have achieved notable successes nationally and internationally for over 100 years, reflecting our strong sporting culture.

However, it is important to recognise that winning is not the only measure of success. If this were the case then only a small number of participants would gain real satisfaction from their involvement in sport. In this book, *Success from Within*, Brendan Hackett shows conclusively that performing to the best of one's ability is a true measure of success. If sports participants focus on their own performance and the factors they can control and influence, they have a greater chance of reaching their goals.

This principle can apply to all sports participants. If one has the talent of Catherina McKiernan in athletics; Tiger Woods in golf; an inter-county player in football, hurling or camogie; or an international player in other sports; the actual level of performance will be very high. However, for those who are not blessed with such talent the principle of being the best you can be also applies.

Success From Within

In educating coaches the National Coaching and Training Centre (NCTC) has developed three major modules, dealing with *The Sport, The Participant* and *The Coach*. Within *The Sport* module, a model that is used by many sports to analyse and develop performance includes Technical, Tactical, Physical and Mental components. A central element of the module *The Participant* deals with mental fitness, highlighting the centrality of the psychological elements of performance. Through its work the NCTC has identified the area of mental fitness as an element of sports performance where major improvements can be achieved. It is also recognised that the elements of mental fitness must be fully understood and applied by successful coaches.

This book focuses on the area of mental fitness and how it can be integrated across all the areas of preparation in sport. It will assist participants and coaches to set realistic and attainable goals, identify needs in the area of mental fitness; develop mental fitness techniques and how to include them in training, and competitive situations.

These steps will allow each participant to improve their performance and move closer to their full potential. The book will be of benefit to all participants: top performers, those at club level, and developing young players and athletes. The approach taken by Brendan Hackett will allow each participant to experience success at a level appropriate to his or her ability and goals.

The focus of this book strongly complements the work of the NCTC. The central mission of the Centre is to support the development of performance and coaching. The Centre has formed partnerships with other organisations and agencies with the aim of putting in place a world class sports system for Irish sport. A number of initiatives have been undertaken by the Centre in the context of the policies of the Irish Sports Council and the Department of Tourism, Sports and Recreation. These initiatives include:

- **The National Coaching Development Programme:** At the core of the Programme is a 4 level coaching ladder, going from beginner coach at level 1 to international level coach at level 4. The Programme has been implemented to-date in 28 sports, with an involvement of over 15,000 coaches. The identification, recruitment, education and deployment of coaches will continue to form a central focus for the second cycle of the programme, beginning in 1999.

- **Player/Athlete Support Initiatives:** NCTC provides direct physiological, medical and nutritional support to 600 players and athletes on an annual basis. Recently NCTC has played a central role in developing the new International Carding Scheme for Ireland's world class and talented young players and athletes. As part of the scheme NCTC will co-ordinate the Sports Science and Medical Support Network which will provide support to these players and athletes.

- **National Sports Information Service:** Information on all aspects of sport is available through a customised information service at the NCTC.

- **Sports Village:** NCTC has established high quality residential training facilities on the campus of the University of Limerick on a year round basis for squads and athletes to train or to receive sports science and medical support.

Within the context of all these initiatives there is a need to provide resources for coaches, players, athletes and administrators to get the most out of what they do. Brendan Hackett has made an important contribution in this regard through *Success from Within*. The book provides a clear and progressive framework in mental fitness which can be applied by all involved in sport. As such it marks a further important step forward in the growing self-confidence within Irish sport.

The book provides an excellent reference point for all those wishing to develop the mental side of performance within sport. In Ireland, we are only beginning to tap into the power of psychology as it relates to performance. In an era where illicit means of enhancing performance are all too often used, this empowering publication offers hope to all those who still believe in the power of mind, spirit and the legimate pursuit of high performance in sport.

In bringing this publication to you, the NCTC has been pleased once again to co-operate closely with adidas (Irl) Ltd. adidas have clearly demonstrated their commitment to helping the long term development of Irish sport through their foresighted and synergistic team work with NCTC. In this case, we can thank Brendan Hackett and adidas for helping us all to realise that success truly does come from within – a success which we can all achieve with the right approach.

Pat Duffy
Director
National Coaching and Training Centre

CONTENTS

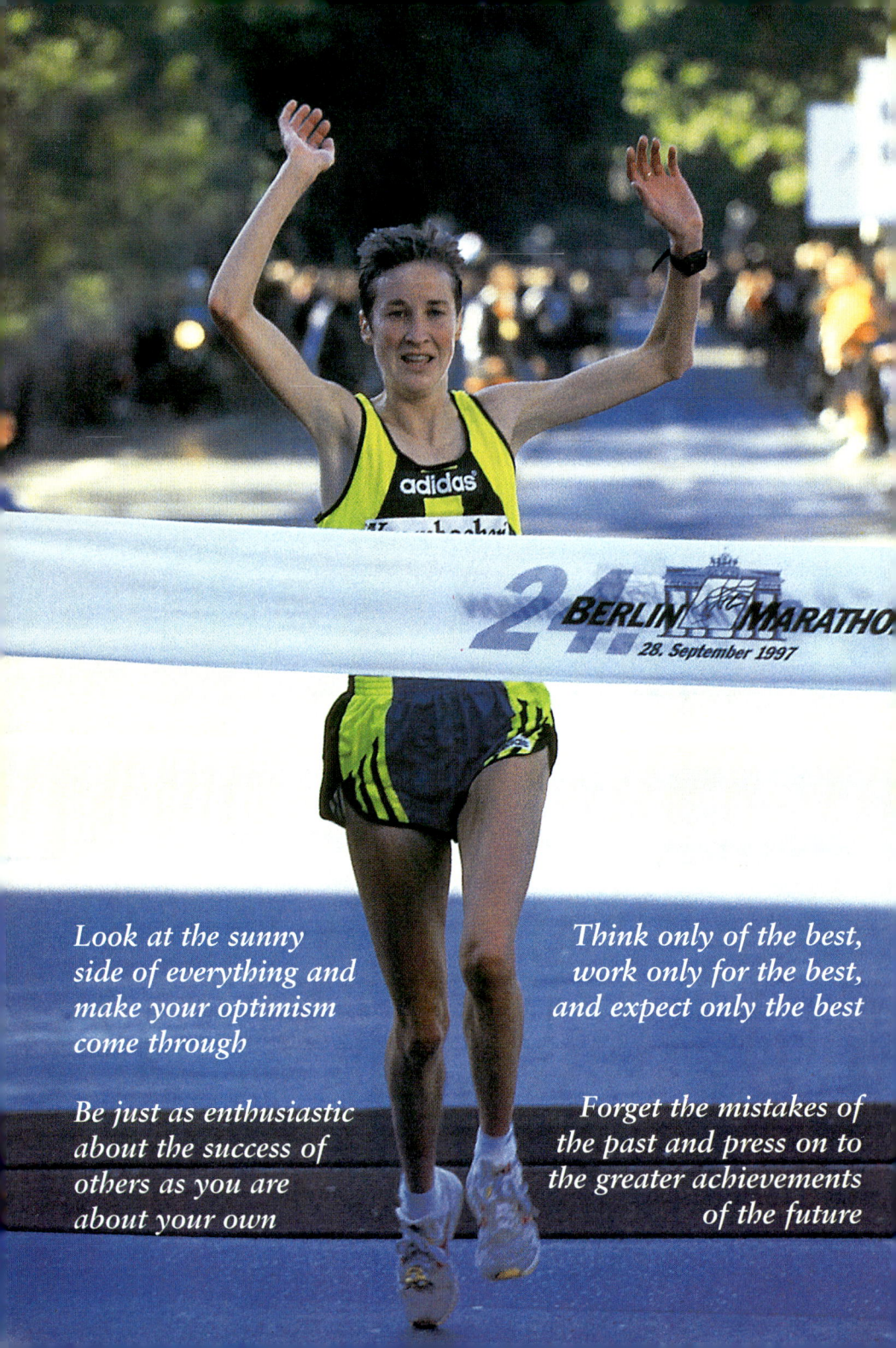

Look at the sunny
side of everything and
make your optimism
come through

Be just as enthusiastic
about the success of
others as you are
about your own

Think only of the best,
work only for the best,
and expect only the best

Forget the mistakes of
the past and press on to
the greater achievements
of the future

INTRODUCTION

Throughout my life, I have been fascinated by success. When I see or hear about people achieving their dreams, rising to meet a challenge, or performing to their potential, particularly under pressure, I am moved. It is sporting success, however, that has always touched me most.

Thanks to a combination of education, personal experience, and the privilege of having worked closely with some remarkable people, I have come to understand what it takes to succeed in sport. As a coach and, more recently, a sports consultant, I have been trying for almost 20 years to help people achieve success in a variety of endeavours. Along the way, my perception of what is meant by success and the process of attaining it has expanded greatly. Over the years I have shared many of my ideas at coaching courses, seminars, and in magazine articles. This book is an attempt to pass on this accumulated knowledge in the belief that it will help a wider audience.

The first thing to be said about this book is that it is aimed at sportspeople and coaches of all types and at all levels. In the first chapter I define what I mean by sporting success – it is essentially being the best that you can be. I now recognise that performing to your potential is a combination of many factors. This was not always my belief. As a competitor and later as a physical education student, I used to believe the way to get better at sport was through skill practice and physical training. In college, I developed an appreciation that tactical awareness was also a factor in sporting success.

I began coaching gaelic football during my college years, and these beliefs formed the basis of my coaching philosophy. I tried to plan training so that players got as much skill practice as possible in the time available; and I strongly emphasised physical fitness. I also preached tactical awareness – but did not give it the same attention as fitness training or skills practice. The Thomond College team that I coached was highly successful. They were talented to begin with, but I felt that the type of training they were doing was the major reason for their success. The training was of course a big factor – but it took me a few more years to learn that there were other parts to the jigsaw of sporting success. While at college I coached other, less successful, teams. But since I did not have overall control of their training, I assumed their comparative failure was a result of neglect of other aspects of preparation.

After college, the natural progression was club and ultimately county. I was fortunate to manage a county team at the relatively young age of 26. Appointed manager of Longford in 1987, I still believed strongly that the route to success was a combination of physical fitness, skill, and tactical awareness. Longford, a Division 3 team, were soon winning games under the new regime. And when they gained promotion, I was further convinced I was on the right road.

Summer approached and Longford had reached a provincial semi-final for the first time in 18 years. They faced Dublin, one of the strongest teams in the country. I was confident we would surprise everyone with our fitness, skill, and tactical wisdom. At half time, with Longford leading by three points, my confidence had grown to total conviction. The next 35 minutes changed my sporting philosophy forever. When Dublin drew level with 20 minutes remaining, a change came over my team: they became overwhelmed, they froze, they gave up, they looked like a team that had never trained together. They eventually lost by 18 points.

I was astonished and baffled. What had happened? They were fit enough. They couldn't suddenly become less skillful, could they? We all took a break for a few weeks, in which time I reviewed the training plans. I could find no obvious fault – maybe it had been just one of those days. I looked forward to the new season and the challenge of Division 2.

I rang all the players and arrived to the first training session, optimistic, positive, energetic, and confident. I was greeted by the not-so-grand total of six players. In fact there were more officials than footballers. What was wrong? Why weren't the team feeling as I did? At last it dawned on me – the attitudes and emotions of many of the players were entirely different to my own. Never before had I come across such palpable despondency, negativity, embarrassment, pessimism, doubt, insecurity, and apathy.

I had always assumed everyone in sport had the same attitudes I had – commitment, determination, confidence, resolve, delight in challenge, thirst for knowledge, optimism. How had I developed a mindset like this? Was it genetic? Until then, I had never pondered the question.

My earliest sporting heroes were from soccer. I imitated players from England and Brazil as I played. But it was the success of a broad range of Irish sportspeople both at home and abroad that really inspired me. Without realising it, I was imbibing their outlook. I didn't have their physical talents, but I was learning mental qualities from them. I am not saying heredity played no part, but I was unconsciously learning about mental fitness. My parents, teachers, and friends also contributed greatly to my developing this successful mindset.

When I started competing at sports, I was blessed with coaches who were unique. I say unique because I now see that they enhanced my mental fitness by their methods and their underlying philosophies. They instilled confidence, discipline, and self-control. They deepened my love for sport, and I looked forward to training and competing.

Unfortunately, not all who take up sport are so fortunate. Over the years I have met so many people whose mental fitness was undermined if not destroyed by negative coaching. Many of these people no longer play or compete – and those of them who have persisted are still trying years later to develop aspects of their mental fitness.

My experience was so much different. I played on teams that enjoyed more success than failure. And there was always the underlying philosophy that doing your best was what really mattered. Sometimes we were beaten by better opponents, but if we could say 'I performed to the best of my ability on the day', then we had been successful. When I entered college, my mental fitness was already well developed. I took this for granted, because those around me were all of similar mind. Eight years later, as Longford collapsed to Dublin, I was confronted with the reality: mental fitness was by no means universal; it varied greatly from person to person; background, education, and associates all contributed to the discrepancies. I came to a decisive conclusion: mental fitness was just as necessary as physical fitness, skill, and tactical awareness in reaching one's potential.

Over a number of years, through study, experience, and experiment, I had deepened my understanding of physical fitness. As I faced into my second year with Longford I had come to appreciate the role of the mind in sporting performance. I realised that mental fitness needed the same attention as the physical, tactical or technical aspects of preparation. The problem I faced was one of turning this into action.

In 1988 mental fitness was not as familiar a topic in Ireland as it is today. Books on the subject were rare, and the media seldom referred to it. I remembered attending a lecture on sports psychology at a coaching conference. I looked back over the notes and this prompted me to find out more about this topic. I began to accumulate books from abroad, and when the odd title appeared in Dublin I would snap it up. I was becoming more interested in the role of the mind in sport. I tried things out with players – some worked, some fell flat. In the next couple of years I could see that this aspect of sport was underestimated and I didn't have the knowledge or experience to help players sufficiently.

In 1990, at a time when I was considering doing a postgraduate degree in sports psychology, I travelled with the Irish Compromise Rules team to Australia. On that trip I visited universities and sports academies at which psychologists were part of the backroom teams for most sports. These sports psychologists enjoyed the same standing as the conditioning coaches, the skills coaches, the tactical advisors, and the physiotherapists.

Soon after returning home, I was fortunate to receive a postgraduate scholarship under an initiative set up by the University of Limerick and the Gaelic Athletic Association. I studied sports psychology. Sports psychology is a very broad field, but my focus was on understanding the role of mental factors in sporting performance, and the development of methods to improve these qualities. I refer to these as mental fitness. Since graduating in 1993 I have worked as a sports consultant, combining mental fitness with the other elements of preparation to help people reach their potential. I work with individual sportspeople, teams, coaches and organisations at all levels in a variety of sports.

To some, the mention of mental fitness or psychology in the context of sport suggests hocus-pocus; others dismiss as weakminded the competitor who needs such mental training. But that prejudice is changing fast. In recent years, many individuals and teams have testified to the benefits of working with psychologists and mental trainers. In Ireland notable examples include Derry (All Ireland Football Champions 1993), Wexford (All Ireland Hurling Champions 1996), boxer Michael Carruth (Olympic Champion 1992) and professional golfer Padraig Harrington (World Cup Champion 1997).

Success in sport is within everybody's reach, but without a balanced programme of preparation that includes working on your mental fitness it will be difficult to perform to your best – consistently. For too long competitive temperament has been deemed unchangeable, a factor of individual personality, and therefore outside the reach of training. As I say, this misconception is changing rapidly. It is my hope that this book will accelerate the speed of change. The central messages in this book are:

Mental fitness is an essential ingredient in sporting performances.

It can be developed through practice particularly if it is integrated into your overall training programme.

You can improve your mental fitness at any age at whatever level of sport you participate in.

I wish you well in your chosen sport and hope this book contributes in some way to your success in that sport.

Chapter 1

STEPS TO SUCCESS

SPORTING SUCCESS

THE SUCCESS JIGSAW

ELEMENTS OF SUCCESS

MENTAL FITNESS

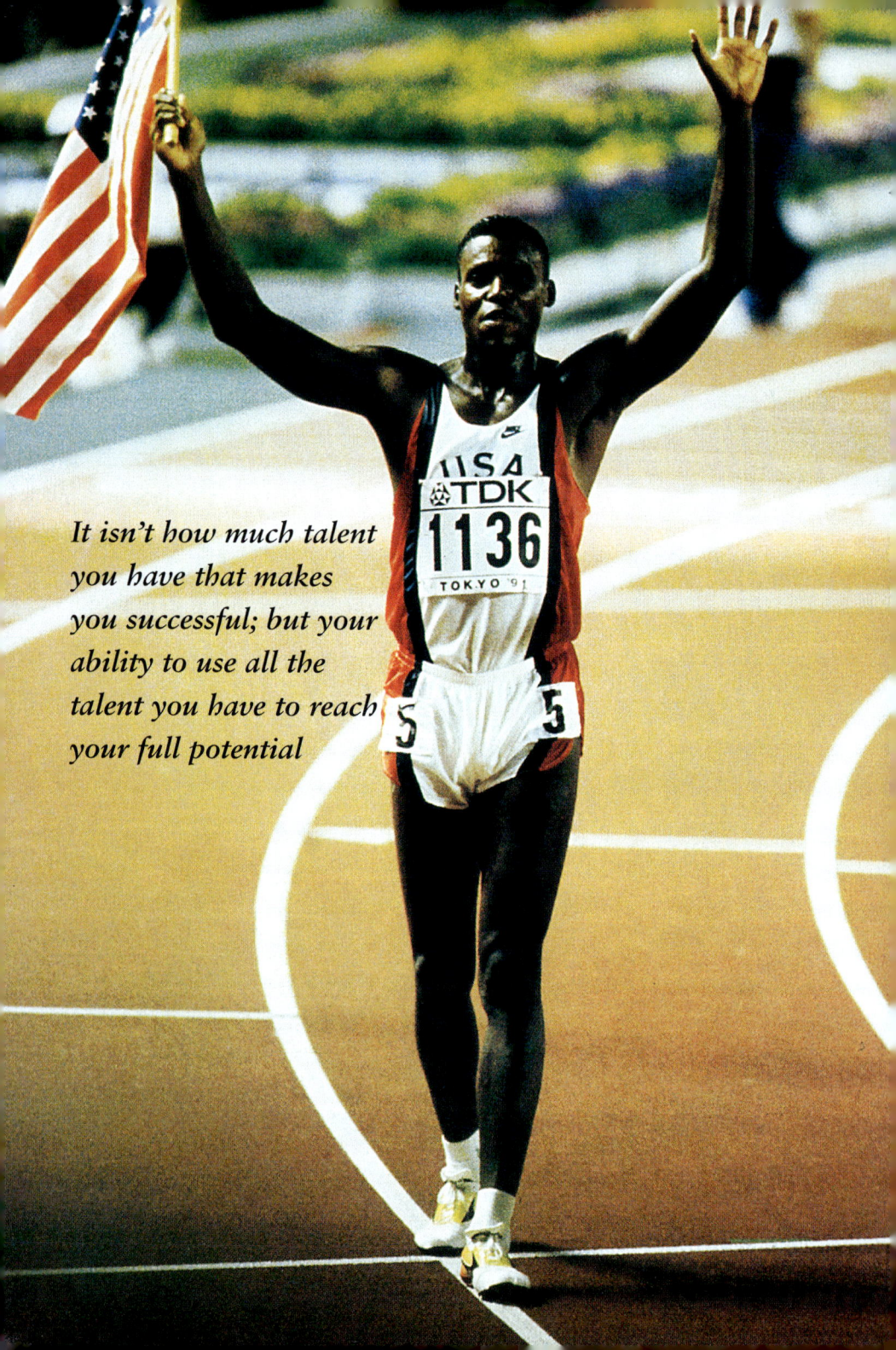

It isn't how much talent you have that makes you successful; but your ability to use all the talent you have to reach your full potential

"It isn't how much talent you have that makes you successful; but your ability to use all the talent you have to reach your full potential."
(Carl Lewis, winner of ten Olympic Gold Medals.)

"You could be the world's best garbage man, the world's best model; it doesn't matter what you do as long as you give it your best."
(Muhammad Ali, Olympic and World Heavyweight Boxing Champion.)

Everyone desires success – especially those involved in sport. For many, success means winning. But success is about more than winning; it is about being the best you can be – performing at or close to your potential no matter what your talent or the level at which you play your chosen sport. Success is about achieving your goals. That can mean bettering your own performance, beating a particular opponent, reaching a target, or simply competing to the best of your ability. Many factors contribute to sporting success. This book focuses on one of them – mental fitness. As the following pages will make clear, mental fitness is just one piece in the jigsaw of sporting success. But it is such an important piece that it is difficult to be truly successful without it.

The ensuing chapters will look in detail at mental fitness and present many ideas on how to achieve it. Strategies to develop mental fitness have been used by sports people and coaches since sport began. In many instances the process by which these methods have been learned has been lengthy and largely through trial and error. This book aims to draw on the experience of successful sportspeople and hasten this learning process. Developing mental fitness through the use of tried and tested methods is like 'putting an old head on young shoulders'. You will see that much of the information and many of the suggestions are commonsense. Yet for most sportspersons they are not common practice.

Opposite: Carl Lewis

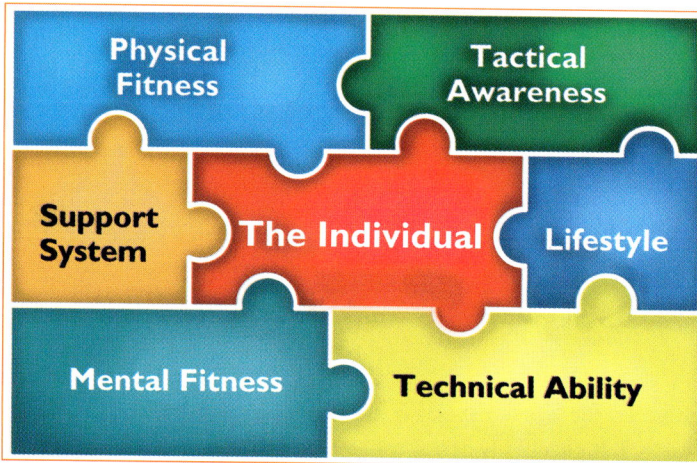

The central piece in this jigsaw is the individual. Each of us has been shaped by a unique blend of innate qualities, intelligence, experiences, and influences. Understanding this uniqueness is essential when trying to build the jigsaw.

Putting the jigsaw pieces together requires a combination of experience, training, coaching, and education. Information, in the form of scientific knowledge, about the various jigsaw pieces is more plentiful and more readily available now than it has ever been. Yet much of this information is often overlooked or ignored, especially the information relating to the jigsaw piece called **mental fitness**.

Even though we are concerned in this book mainly with mental fitness, we will do well to look briefly at the other factors that contribute to success in sport. To neglect any one of them is to limit your chances of being the best you can be.

ELEMENTS OF SUCCESS

1. PHYSICAL FITNESS

Physical fitness is not so much a single, discrete quality as a combination of several components. These components each describe a distinct capability. The terms used to describe these components tell you a good deal – the chief among them being the Four **S**s: **stamina**, **strength**, **speed**, **suppleness**.

STAMINA
the ability to sustain an effort or repeated efforts over a period of time.

STRENGTH
the ability to exert force, as in lifting, resisting, pulling and pushing.

SPEED
the ability to move quickly, as in sprinting.

SUPPLENESS
the ability to move joints and muscles through their full ranges of motion. Also called flexibility.

Researchers describe other components of physical fitness, such as agility, balance, co-ordination, power, reaction time, physique, and body composition. Even though genetics ultimately determines your physical potential, each of these elements of fitness can be improved to varying degrees through regular training. For that training to be most effective it must be planned and follow certain guiding principles. A number of guiding steps for the implementation of physical training are outlined on the following pages.

STEPS IN IMPLEMENTING A PHYSICAL TRAINING PROGRAMME.

ASSESS

What are the physical demands of your sport? Too often people train without asking themselves what they are trying to develop. Examine your sport and consider what components of physical fitness are most appropriate to it. Some sports require emphasis on one aspect of fitness, for example, marathon running demands stamina, weightlifting demands strength. Most sports, however, require a balance of all aspects of fitness. Assessments such as laboratory tests or simple field tests are then useful to determine individual strengths and weaknesses.

BE SPECIFIC

Having assessed your fitness and established which components of fitness you need to concentrate on, select the appropriate type of training. It may be that you have a coach and that your fitness programme is devised for you. But if you are training on your own, you may need to seek help. Remember, not all training is effective. You could be wasting much time and effort and even causing injury through inappropriate training.

PLAN

Planning ensures that training is effective and progressive. To be effective, training must place a suitable demand on your body based on your current level of fitness. This training stimulus is usually called an overload. Your training programme should dictate how often you train (frequency), how hard you train (intensity), how long you train (duration), and how much you train (volume). For example a runner may train 6 days per week (frequency). The intensity can vary; two of those days may be at race pace (90 - 100% effort), two at medium pace (80% effort) and two at easy pace (60-70% effort). The duration can vary from session to session. The volume refers to the overall amount of training. Runners usually measure this in miles per week. Sometimes planning is referred to as the FITT principle. F (frequency) I (intensity) T (time or duration) and T (type) of training.

The body adapts to the added demands of training. To ensure this adaptation is progressive and to avoid injury or staleness it is necessary to vary the training stimulus. This is achieved by changing the emphasis of the frequency, intensity, duration, or volume of training.

RECOVER

It is during the recovery phase that many of the adaptations occur. A training programme should also take into account that recovery is essential.
Effective training + recovery = improved fitness.
Hard work needs to be balanced with recovery if progress is to be maintained.

MONITOR

Monitoring identifies the effectiveness of the training programme. It can also highlight the degree of reversibility after an absence from training. The adaptations that occur from training are reversible if training ceases. The rates of individual adaptation and reversibility vary greatly and therefore need constant monitoring.

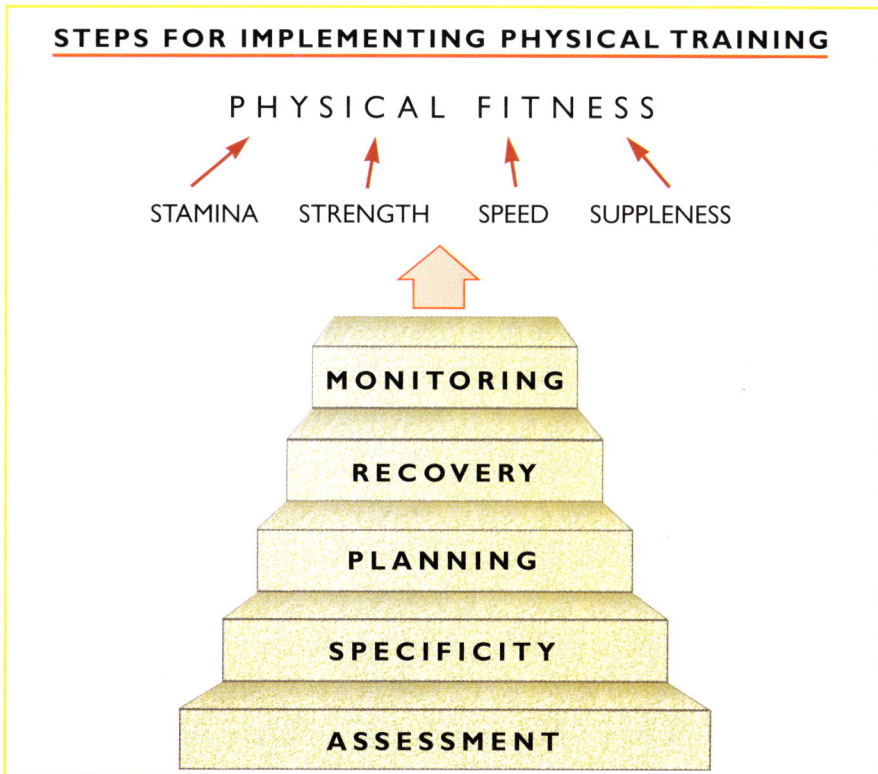

STEPS FOR IMPLEMENTING PHYSICAL TRAINING

P H Y S I C A L   F I T N E S S

STAMINA   STRENGTH   SPEED   SUPPLENESS

MONITORING

RECOVERY

PLANNING

SPECIFICITY

ASSESSMENT

2. TECHNICAL ABILITY

Can you think of any sport in which it is possible to be successful without some proficiency in the basic skills? As with most of the other success elements, everybody has a different degree of ability to start with. Your technical ability, no matter what your sport, can be improved through practice. Regular and correct practice is the basis of becoming more proficient and skilled.

The emphasis is on regularity and effectiveness. The key to learning most skills is repetition. Some people are more gifted than others, but it is repetition that makes the skill consistent. If that weren't so why do elite sportspersons practise so much? Surely after playing the game for a number of years they wouldn't need to. Not so. It's the constant repetition that ensures they can reproduce their skills time and again even under intense pressure – 'practice makes permanent'.

For practice to be effective you must be practising the correct technique under the right conditions. The old saying 'practice makes perfect' is not very helpful because if you practise something incorrectly you become proficient at doing it wrongly. Better to follow the principle 'perfect practice makes perfect and permanent'. So, when practising and developing the technical aspects of your sport, pay attention to what and how you are practising.

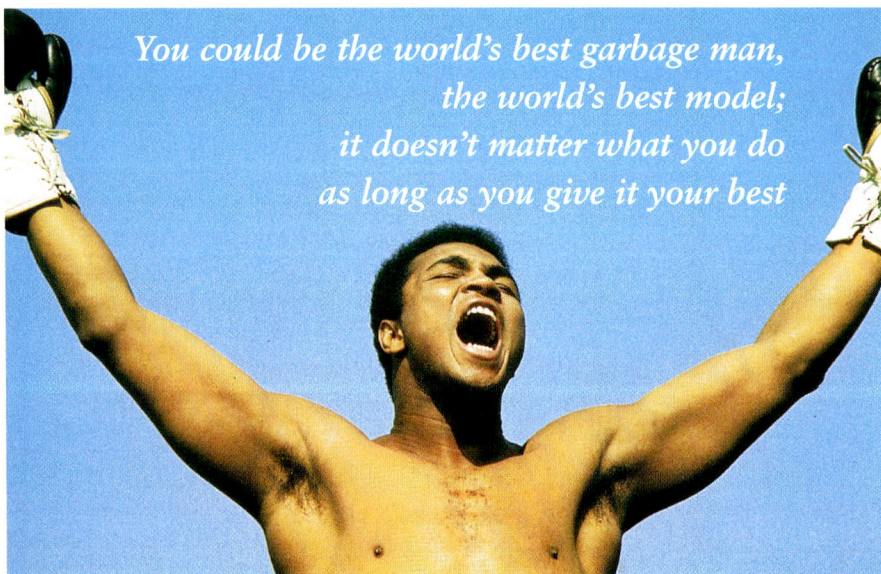

You could be the world's best garbage man,
the world's best model;
it doesn't matter what you do
as long as you give it your best

3. TACTICAL AWARENESS

Nearly all sports have a tactical element to them. A variety of attacking and defensive formations are part of team sports. Sports that involve racing offer tactical options such as leading, sitting back or changing pace at various stages. In many instances it is left up to the individual to somehow develop such awareness through trial and error. You hear statements such as 'He's a great reader of the game', 'She always seems to be in the right place at the right time', 'He's a great judge of pace', 'They seem to be one move ahead of their opponents'. Utterances like these suggest that sportspeople and coaches see tactical awareness as an innate gift.

Good coaching can help you develop tactical awareness. The coach can set up practices that replicate competitive situations and teach players their role in the play. When the players come to know what is expected of them, the situations can be made more difficult and the players encouraged to make their own decisions. The same applies to individual sports. Tactical awareness can be taught through demonstration, setting up appropriate experiences and providing feedback to the performer. It is an essential part of the coaching process.

4. SUPPORT SYSTEM

Performing to your best is so much easier when you are well supported. The key people in terms of support are family, coaches, teachers, clubmates, sports scientists, medics, sponsors, friends, officials, national governing bodies and the media. These people provide feedback, coaching, facilities, equipment and finance. A good support system is conducive to playing to your potential.

5. LIFESTYLE

Your lifestyle, and the way you manage it, bears heavily on how you perform. For example, adequate rest and a balanced diet are essential to performing well. Here are some suggestions that can help to make your lifestyle more manageable:

Opposite: Muhammad Ali

REST

The most obvious form of rest is sleep. If you have a busy schedule and are engaged in regular training, a good night's sleep is vital. Eight hours is the usual requirement, but take as much as you need to recover. A 20-minute nap in the afternoon or just after work can revitalise you. We mentioned rest already in relation to physical training. Apart from regular rest days, you may need to cut back on training if you are busy at work, have exams, or are going through any kind of crisis. If you keep pushing on all fronts you will end up drained. Be alert for the signals that tell you to cut back, such as loss of form, tiredness, injury, or illness.

DIET

A balanced diet containing sufficient energy and a suitable variety of nutrients is vital to performance in sport. Fortunately, information is now widely and readily available on how to balance your diet and ensure that you have all the recommended nutrients. Health promotion agencies distribute useful guidelines. Remember, fluid intake is also an integral part of a balanced diet.

RELAXATION

Any activity that replenishes your energy and refreshes you can be considered relaxation. Passive forms of relaxation include massage, soaking in the bath, and listening to music. Active forms include light stretching, easy walking (preferably in a scenic area), going to the cinema, reading, and relaxation training.

STRESS

When a person is over-extending for a prolonged period of time he or she can become stressed. Stress is not easy to define because people react differently to situations. Although the causes may be varied the symptoms are very similar. Being overstressed affects physical, mental, and emotional function. The signs include tiredness, loss of form, and mood swings – whenever you detect any or all of these, act quickly to restore the balance as soon as possible.

The remedy for stress is regular recuperation. Pay more attention to relaxation activities to balance the stress of training and a busy lifestyle. The big problem for most people is that stress creeps up on them and they are often the last to realise what is happening. Sportspeople have the added burden that they are pushing themselves physically, on top of the normal stresses that are part and parcel of life.

Being understressed is not a condition that is associated with sportspeople – but it can be just as destructive as its opposite. The most obvious state of physical understress is inactivity, usually due to injury. Persons used to high levels of physical exertion can have real difficulty adjusting to a lengthy lay-off. Another form of understress is lack of mental stimulation. A life with little challenge will tend to undermine anybody. Individuals who become unemployed or work in boring jobs are vulnerable to understress. This can impact on the self-esteem and confidence that are necessary for optimum performance.

6. MENTAL FITNESS

The sixth element in the jigsaw of sporting success is mental fitness. All of the other elements contribute significantly to optimum performance. But this book is written in the belief that mental fitness is the element that offers the greatest opportunity for improved performance – not least because it is usually the most neglected element. In most sporting contests the competitors' level of physical fitness is similar. The differences in skill and tactical understanding can be minimal, so it is often mental factors that account for the differences between teams or individuals in the competitive arena. Many sportspersons acknowledge that mental factors play a significant part in success, but they are not so sure how to develop them.

The assumption too often is that mental fitness is inherent, part of a person's make-up and therefore not part of preparation like physical training or skill work. We hear phrases like:
'he lacks the bottle'
'she loses the head'
'they haven't got the heart'
'he can't handle the pressure'
'they have a great tradition'
'she's a great battler'

These statements are indicative of this assumption. As you read through this book you will see that mental fitness can be developed and improved upon just like the other elements in the success jigsaw. The major premise of this work is that, if we can articulate what mental factors or qualities make successful performers special then we can teach others these mental qualities necessary to perform to their best more consistently.

So what is mental fitness? How does it influence performance? Can it be improved?

The final section of this chapter describes mental fitness. Subsequent chapters examine how various aspects of mental fitness influence performance and present ideas on how to improve them. In attempting to understand mental fitness there are three rich sources of information. Each of these areas has been thoroughly researched and provides invaluable insights into the role of mental factors in sport.

The psychological differences between successful and unsuccessful sportspersons

The general findings show that successful people have higher self confidence, report fewer doubts, are more positive, experience imagery more likely to portray successful performance, are better able to control and utilise anxiety, and have high levels of concentration. They are also more persistent and prepare more thoroughly.

What it takes to 'make it'

Researchers have interviewed successful athletes, coaches, and talent scouts to find out what are the qualities that go hand-in-hand with success. The qualities most commonly cited are commitment, confidence, self-control and concentration.

Commitment covers such things as ambition, the desire or dream to achieve, persistence to train long and hard, willingness to make sacrifices, and the ability to plan, correct, and take advice. Self-control entails the ability to maintain composure, contain anxiety, stay positive, accept criticism, and meet failure stoically.

Champions' descriptions of peak performances

When winners at sport are asked to describe epic performances, there are remarkable similarities. The following description is a composite put together by sport psychologist Jim Loehr, based on thousands of interviews he conducted with sportspeople from numerous disciplines.

"I felt physically relaxed, but really energised and pumped up. I experienced no anxiety or fear, and the whole experience was totally enjoyable. I experienced a very real sense of calmness and quiet inside, and everything just seemed to flow automatically. I didn't really think about what I was supposed to do: it just seemed to happen naturally. Even though I was really hustling, it was all very effortless. I always seemed to have enough time and energy and rarely felt rushed. I felt like I could do almost anything, as if I were in complete control. I felt really confident and positive. It also seemed very easy to concentrate. I was totally tuned into what I was doing. I was aware of everything but distracted by nothing. It almost seemed like I knew what was going to happen before it actually did."

The reflections below also highlight mental qualities of successful people.

Winners v Losers

When a winner makes a mistake, he says, "I was wrong;"
When a loser makes a mistake, he says, "It wasn't my fault."
A winner works harder than a loser and has more time;
A loser is always too busy to do what is necessary.
A winner goes through a problem;
A loser goes around it, and never gets past it.
A winner makes commitments;
A loser makes promises.
A winner says, "I'm good, but not as good as I ought to be;"
A loser says, "I'm not as bad as a lot of other people."

A winner listens;
A loser just waits until it is his turn to talk.
A winner respects those who are superior to him and tries to learn
something from them;
A loser resents those who are superior to him and tries
to find chinks in their armour.
A winner feels responsible for more than his job;
A loser says, "I only work here."
A winner says "There ought to be a better way to do it;"
A loser says "That's the way it's always been done here."

COMPONENTS OF MENTAL FITNESS

These areas of research show that to consistently produce your best, certain psychological qualities are just as important as physical qualities and abilities. These qualities are referred to in this book as the components of mental fitness. Some authors refer to them as mental skills. The four main components are:

COMMITMENT

is the effort and energy that goes into turning goals into reality.

CONFIDENCE

is the belief that you have the abilities or resources to meet the demands of situations you are likely to face.

CONTROL

is taking charge of the mental processes to create an internal environment that is conducive to performing well.

CONCENTRATION

is the ability to direct your attention to relevant cues and maintain your attention for the appropriate amount of time.

These components are not static traits. They can be modified, developed, and improved, just like the components of physical fitness. Individuals may be gifted in one or more of these aspects, but improvement is possible in everyone. People may, and often do, employ the techniques that develop the Four Cs without actually realising it. Successful people have developed their mental fitness to a level that has contributed to their success, and you can learn how to do this also.

The process by which mental fitness is deliberately developed is referred to as mental or psychological training. It is also described as performance enhancement. Mental training consists of using a combination of methods, strategies and interventions on a consistent basis to improve, modify and enhance one or more of the components of mental fitness. Some of the most common methods used by sportspeople and coaches to enhance mental fitness include goal-setting, competition planning, relaxation and imagery. The steps for implementing a mental training programme have been adapted from the physical training guidelines described on pages 18 and 19.

STEPS IN IMPLEMENTING A MENTAL TRAINING PROGRAMME

AWARENESS

Creating awareness of mental fitness and its role in performance is the starting point of any mental training programme. This can be done through guided reading, attending seminars on the topic and listening to appropriate interviews with elite performers in which they make reference to the importance of mental fitness. Awareness can also be created in individuals or teams by asking them to reflect on their preparation and recent performances.

The following awareness exercises can be done on your own or guided by a coach. It is helpful to write down your reflections after each exercise. These and other reflective exercises throughout the book are best done in a quiet environment when you are relaxed and focused.

EXERCISE 1.1 **How do you rate mental fitness?**

Using the six elements in the success jigsaw on page 16 rate each of them out of ten in importance as an ingredient to performing consistently well in your sport. Then calculate how much time and attention you give to each in a normal week. Usually mental fitness will be given a high rating, but on reflection it will be discovered that very little time or attention is given to it compared to the other aspects.

EXERCISE 1.2 **Best v worst performance**

Recall an event when you performed to the best of your ability and reflect on your state of mind that day. Recall a day when you performed poorly. You will notice that there is a marked difference in your two states of mind. This helps draw attention to the role of mental fitness.

EXERCISE 1.3 **What makes them special?**

Consider the difference between successful and unsuccessful sportspeople that you know in terms of their mental fitness. Successful people are defined as those who perform at or close to their potential on a consistent basis. Make a list of the mental characteristics or qualities of successful performers. This also highlights the importance of mental fitness.

ASSESS

Assessment also creates awareness and helps form the basis of a mental training programme. Assess both the sport and the performer at the outset. An examination of the demands of a sport will indicate the mental fitness components most essential to consistent performance in that sport. Having established the significance of each of these, the next step is to assess yourself or the people you coach in each of these aspects of mental fitness. There are many suggestions in each chapter on how to do this. Your own observations and those of your coach are the most basic forms of assessment. Observe training sessions and competitions, use questionnaires or interviews to build up a profile of yourself or your athletes' mental fitness. The acronym BASIC is a useful guideline. This involves assessing a person in the following areas: behaviour, affect, sensations, imagery and cognitions.

Behaviour:

Overt behaviour is a good starting point because it is observable. Behaviour at training and during competitions reveals a great deal about a person's state of mind. Here are some examples of typical behaviours and their possible significance.

Strong Commitment
show enthusiasm
practise diligently
perform to potential consistently
take action

Poor Commitment
lack of enthusiasm
poor attendance at training
give up when falling behind
complain frequently

Strong Confidence
positive posture
take responsibility
talk about abilities not limitations

Poor Confidence
bored or negative appearance
play defensively or tentatively
talk about limitations

Strong Control
relaxed, unafraid
composed under pressure
consistent performer

Poor Control
anxious, fearful
losing composure
inconsistent, often better in training

Strong Concentration
focused on the task
unaffected by distraction

Poor Concentration
easily distracted
shows signs of frustration

To form a more complete picture it is best to back up observation with an interview so that clarification can be sought if necessary. Some behaviours can be indicative of a problem in one or two areas. For example, making uncharacteristic mistakes in the early stages of a competition could be due to anxiety, lack of concentration, feelings of low confidence on the day, or a combination of all of them. Discussion between coach and performers will clarify observations.

Affect:

This means paying attention to feelings and moods. These may be expressed through behaviour but often they are not. So taking time to ask a person about his or her feelings could be very beneficial in assessing areas that might need attention. Feelings such as fear, anxiety, anger, and depression have an impact in sporting performance.

Sensations:

Elicit information on body sensations. It should be noticed if sensations are associated with a particular behaviour or emotion. For example a number of bodily functions are affected by anxiety such as heart rate and urinary function.

Imagery:

Identify images that may interfere with performance. An athlete may be pre-programming failure through constantly imagining a particular opponent as unbeatable or replaying an error over and over in the mind. On the other hand, somebody may be good at imagining success or mentally rehearsing for competitions. The ability to use imagery to your advantage is a key part of control.

Cognitions:

These are thoughts, ideas, opinions, and beliefs, and they have a profound effect on all the components of mental fitness. When individuals or teams share their thoughts it can give an insight into their confidence levels as well as the extent to which they are in control. C can also stand for communication. Breakdowns in communication or problematic relationships with significant others can often affect aspects of mental fitness. For example, a coach can undermine a player's confidence through negative comments. The coach may think these comments are motivating the player to greater effort, whereas they can be having the opposite effect.

PLAN

With the information from the assessment, a broad mental training plan can be drawn up. This involves selecting appropriate strategies to develop the relevant components and deciding how and when they will be introduced. Mental training needs to be integrated into the overall preparation. For example, imagery enhances skill training or strategies to develop concentration can be incorporated into tactical training. There is a summary of the mental training strategies on page 142. This is preceded by advice on incorporating mental training into the overall programme. Strategies to address specific needs are shown along with suggestions on how and when these could be introduced throughout a season.

IMPLEMENT

The ultimate success of any programme is that it leads to improved performance when competing. This should be kept in mind at all times when introducing any mental training strategy. Some of the strategies suggested in this book are best introduced off the training ground. For example, drawing up a personal profile to assess your strengths and weaknesses. The off-field exercises may appear theoretical at first, but they are designed to be of benefit in training and on competition day. Many of the exercises are meant to be incorporated into existing training plans. They go hand in hand with physical, technical and tactical training. When you are working on a skill you can also practise concentration techniques. When doing physical training you can work on positive self-talk. Mental training is similar to other aspects of training. Introduce a new strategy slowly and practise it at training sessions where the environment is not too pressurised. Gradually build up the pressure and finally use the strategy in competitive situations.

RE-EVALUATE

The essence of continued improvement is to constantly re-evaluate and draw up new plans or build on your original one if it is bringing rewards. A coach can talk with an athlete, team, or individual player after a competition and ask a number of relevant questions, based on the BASIC format suggested earlier in the section on assessment, to re-evaluate mental fitness and make changes to the training if necessary.

STEPS FOR IMPLEMENTING MENTAL TRAINING

M E N T A L   F I T N E S S

COMMITMENT   CONFIDENCE   CONTROL   CONCENTRATION

RE-EVALUATION

IMPLEMENTATION

PLANNING

ASSESSMENT (BASIC)

CREATE AWARENESS

SUMMARY

Sporting success can be defined as performing to the best of your ability on a consistent basis. You can experience success at any age and in any level of sport if you are willing to prepare thoroughly. Effective preparation means paying attention to six main elements in the success jigsaw; physical fitness, technical ability, tactical awareness, your support system, lifestyle management and mental fitness. This book focuses on mental fitness and shows how it influences sporting performance. The four main components of mental fitness are commitment, confidence, control and concentration. The process by which mental fitness is deliberately developed is referred to as mental training. Mental training is the use of a combination of methods, strategies and interventions on a consistent basis to improve, modify and enhance one or more of the components of mental fitness.

Winners

Winners take chances
Like everyone else they fear failure
but refuse to let fear control them
Winners don't give up
When life gets rough they hang in
until the going gets better
Winners are flexible
They realise there is more than one way
and are willing to try others
Winners know they are not perfect
They respect their weaknesses
while making the most of their strengths
Winners fall but they don't stay down
They stubbornly refuse to let a fall
keep them from climbing
Winners don't blame fate for their failures
Nor luck for their success
Winners accept responsibility for their lives
Winners are positive thinkers
who see good in all things
From the ordinary
they make the extraordinary
Winners believe in the path
they have chosen even when it's hard
Winners are patient
They know a goal is only as worthy
as the effort required to achieve it
Winners are people like you
They make this place a better place to be.

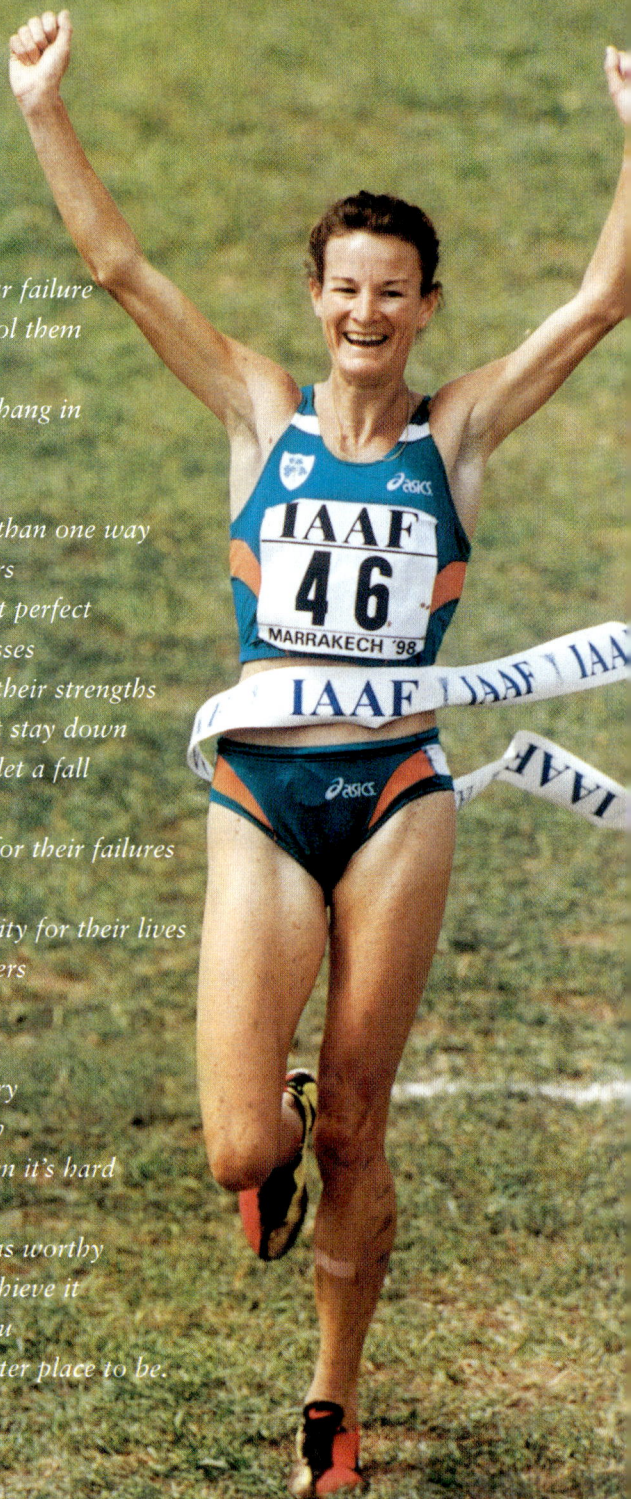

Chapter 2

DEVELOPING COMMITMENT

WHAT IS COMMITMENT?

HOW COMMITTED ARE YOU?

STRATEGIES TO DEVELOP COMMITMENT

IMPLICATIONS FOR COACHES

Opposite: Sonia O'Sullivan, winning the 1998 World Cross Country Championship

Kelly is the kind of guy you just know is out training when you're sitting behind the window on a wet January morning, and even if you got out for two hours with raingear on, he'd have done at least three in shorts with no gloves

"Each great human accomplishment begins with a dream"
(Terry Orlick, sport psychologist.)

"The dictionary is the only place where success comes before work"
(Vince Lombardi, American football coach.)

These two statements go a long way to explain what is meant by commitment. Firstly it is about ambition, desire, an interest or a dream. To turn these feelings and thoughts into reality requires persistence, determination, dedication, drive, willpower, and hard work.

"Nothing in the world can take the place of persistence.
Talent will not; nothing is more common than unsuccessful men with talent.
Genius will not; unrewarded genius is almost a proverb.
Education alone will not; the world is full of educated derelicts.
Persistence and determination alone are omnipotent."
(Ray Croc, founder of McDonalds restaurants.)

This is the same for every sportsperson who wants to be successful. Whether your dream is to run a marathon, improve your golf handicap or win a championship, commitment will be central to your success. Commitment alone does not guarantee success, but without it you will certainly fall short of reaching your potential.

Almost everybody involved in sport has a dream. Why do some people work hard in pursuit of their dream while others give up or simply don't try in the first place? Unfortunately the route to achieving success is a hard one, demanding sacrifice and energy. If it were easy then we would not value our achievements or those of others so highly.

Opposite: Sean Kelly.

Commitment tends to be stronger when the motivation to achieve a dream comes from within. If you are challenged or excited by your goals you are more likely to put in the hard work that is necessary for success. This inner drive seems to be stronger than external motivators such as prizes, prestige, or doing it for others. That is not to say that these external factors are not very important. There are many examples throughout sport of outside forces providing the motivation for outstanding performances. In Gaelic games the pride of the club or county, in rugby the reputation of Munster's battling tradition, in golf the team dimension of the Ryder Cup, in horse racing the desire of the Irish to win at Cheltenham, and in soccer local derbies such as Rangers v Celtic or Everton v Liverpool are just some examples of external factors that provide strong motivation. But this external motivation tends to boost performance in the short term. When you are chasing a dream that requires commitment over a long term a desire from within is a very powerful force.

George O'Connor the Wexford hurler epitomised everything that can be said about commitment. In 1996 after 17 years as a senior player he achieved his lifelong ambition of winning an All Ireland hurling medal. He suffered heartbreaks, injuries, loss of income and countless more setbacks during that long quest. He saw managers and team-mates come and go but he kept coming back each year. He was driven by his dream. From his debut as an 18 year old in 1979 to his career highlight in 1996, George O'Connor devoted enormous time and energy to training and competing. He knew his dream would mean a lot of hard work and persistence, but he was prepared to pay this price to achieve his ultimate goal.

It takes courage to keep committed. Commitment is fuelled by energy. The more intense your desire to be successful, the more energy you will put into achieving your goals. This will influence how often and how hard you train, your persistence to keep going – especially when things get tough, and your determination when you compete.

With commitment, it is a case of actions speak louder than words. You often have to train when you would rather be doing something else. You may have to follow schedules you don't like. You will have to overcome many setbacks, as the road to glory is rarely smooth. You need to stay positive when those around you are often negative. Above all else, you've got to prepare thoroughly for those rare moments of success. Indeed, the preparation takes up nearly all of your time. For those who love competing, patience may also be necessary when you weigh up how much more time is spent training than competing.

Athletes in many disciplines spend 99% of their time training for the couple of hours of actual competition they have during a season. An athlete can spend four years preparing for the Olympics and compete for less than ten minutes if they get there. On the other hand, equally committed athletes often miss major championships by fractions of a second or through illness, having spent years in pursuit of their goal.

This illustrates the point made earlier that commitment will not guarantee success. It is one part of a bigger picture. There is however, a satisfaction in knowing that you gave your best, because it takes courage to commit to being the best that you can be. The majority of people lack this courage. They hold back because of fear of failure. People who are afraid to fail never give total commitment, so they avoid the hurt and risk that results from falling short of their targets. By holding back they have a readymade excuse if things do not work out according to plan. Tennis player Andre Agassi spoke about this fear and how he handles it.

> *"What people want to think, what they want to hope is their business.*
> *I'm just going to play the way I want to play.*
> *I'm not going to be afraid to lose.*
> *If I start worrying about losing, I'll never win."*

Winners are people who make the best of their talents. They use what they have to the fullest capacity no matter what their circumstances are. The great cyclist Sean Kelly is such a person. He is a shining example of what can be achieved through total commitment. A fellow competitor, Robert Millar, was once asked what made Kelly so special. His reply was simple:

> *"Commitment: Kelly is the kind of guy you just know is out training when you're sitting behind the window on a wet January morning, and even if you got out for two hours with raingear on, he'd have done at least three in shorts with no gloves."*

The rest of this chapter looks at commitment in more detail by getting you to evaluate your own commitment and then suggesting some ways of improving it.

The greater the obstacle, the more glory in overcoming it

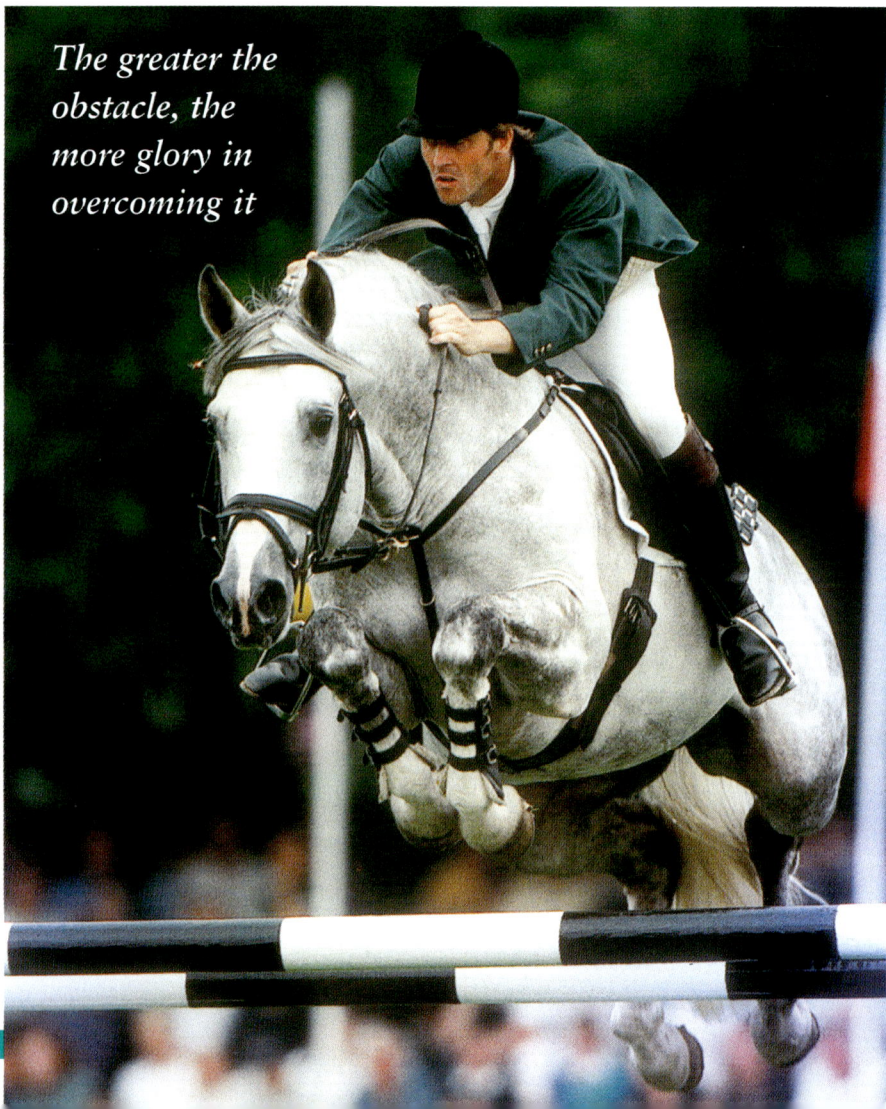

You'll need pen and paper to get the most out of the following exercises. Note that your commitment is being tested already – in being asked to get pen and paper and complete a few exercises you are being challenged.

How interested are you in working on your mental fitness? How much effort are you going to put into improving your mental fitness? The next few pages will help you answer these questions.

So you think you are committed!

Four things can be said of winners:

> they know where they want to go
> they recognise where they are now
> they understand what it is going to take to reach their goal
> they commit themselves to getting there

EXERCISE 2.1   **Where do you want to go?**

Imagine setting out on a journey with no destination in mind – it might be fun for a while, but sooner or later frustration sets in as you journey aimlessly. This often happens in sport. Take a few minutes to consider where you want to go. Close your eyes and visualise your sporting dream. Imagine what you could achieve if you reached your full potential.

Dream Goals

_____

_____

_____

Here are some ideas: to compete in the Olympics; to play for my county team; to win a national medal; to reduce my golf handicap; to ski a black run; to compete again after injury.

Opposite: Trevor Coyle, Irish International show jumper

What would you like to achieve in the coming year? This could be based on your previous season or on the possibilities if you performed to the best of your ability.

Yearly Goals

_____

_____

_____

Some examples: to secure a first-team place; to win a county championship, to take up a new sport.

EXERCISE 2.2 **Where are you now?**

Having established where you would like to go, the next step is to assess where you are now. The process of assessment helps you identify your strengths and weaknesses. In the previous chapter we said that the key to success in sport was a willingness to prepare effectively. A thorough assessment of your current state is of tremendous benefit in guiding your preparations. When you compare where you are now with where you want to go you can begin to draw up a plan of how to get there. The assessment that you carry out now will also be a baseline by which you can monitor your progress in the coming months and years. It may take some time to draw up a full picture of where you are now but it is time well spent.

Personal profile

Drawing up a personal profile is an ideal way to assess where you are now. Whether you are a player or coach, this exercise is invaluable, because the information from it can be used to direct your effort more effectively and efficiently. Do you remember the elements from the success jigsaw? They form the basis of your personal profile. It is possible to assess your current state in each of these elements. Various means of assessment are possible, but the more objective they are, the more accurate the profile will be.

PHYSICAL FITNESS:
Using sophisticated fitness tests in a performance laboratory, field tests, your own observation, or your coach's opinion you can build up a picture of your current levels of fitness. You can assess yourself in each of the components of physical fitness.

TECHNICAL ABILITY:
List the main skills of your sport and then rate yourself on each. Video analysis, coaches' observations, skill tests, and personal opinion are some of the ways to assess technical ability.

TACTICAL AWARENESS:
This tends to be subjective, but the opinion of a coach or 'significant other' should carry much weight.

MENTAL FITNESS:
Just as with physical fitness, you can rate yourself in each component of mental fitness: commitment, confidence, control, and concentration. Your coach's opinion is also important. Observation will be the chief means of assessment.

LIFESTYLE:
An overall picture of your lifestyle can be assembled by assessing the main areas such as diet, rest patterns, impact of work, time management, and general levels of stress.

SUPPORT SYSTEM:
Assess your support by looking at the help you have in relation to the help you need. Refer to such categories as family support, support from work or your school, coaching support, club support, financial support, support from your sports organisation.

Completing the profile

When using objective assessments such as fitness tests, you can use your score directly. When using personal observations or opinions, make sure you rate yourself according to the level you are competing at, or against a target you are aiming for. A system using marks out of ten is useful.

The example below could be a typical player at club level: Each score is a mark out of ten

PHYSICAL	TECHNICAL	TACTICAL	MENTAL	LIFESTYLE	SUPPORT
9	8	8	8	5	8
Stamina	Passing	Support	Commitment	Diet	Family
6	8	6	6	5	8
Strength	Receiving	Creating Space	Confidence	Rest	Friends
8	4	9	7	5	8
Speed	Shooting	Pressure	Control	Work	Coach
4	7	9	5	5	6
Suppleness	Tackling	Covering	Concentration	Stress	Finance

EXERCISE 2.3   **What's it going to take?**

The short answer is commitment. Almost every success story is a tale of the extraordinary lengths to which people go to realise their dream. At the 1976 Olympic Games in Montreal, Nadia Comaneci stunned the world when she produced the first ever perfect score (10 out of 10) in an international gymnastics competition. Over the following four days she produced an astonishing seven perfect scores. When quizzed about her success, she put it simply:

"Hard work. If I work on a certain move constantly, then, finally, it doesn't seem so risky to me. The idea is that the move stays dangerous to my foes, but it is not to me. Hard work has made it easy. That is my secret."

It takes energy to reach your goals, and you have that energy. But if you are like most people, your energy is diffused and spread over many areas of your life. If you want to get the best out of yourself in sport or in pursuit of other dreams, you need to harness most of your energy to that end.

This next exercise, called a *force field analysis*, provides some fascinating insights. It invites you to examine the forces that affect you as you try to pursue your dream.

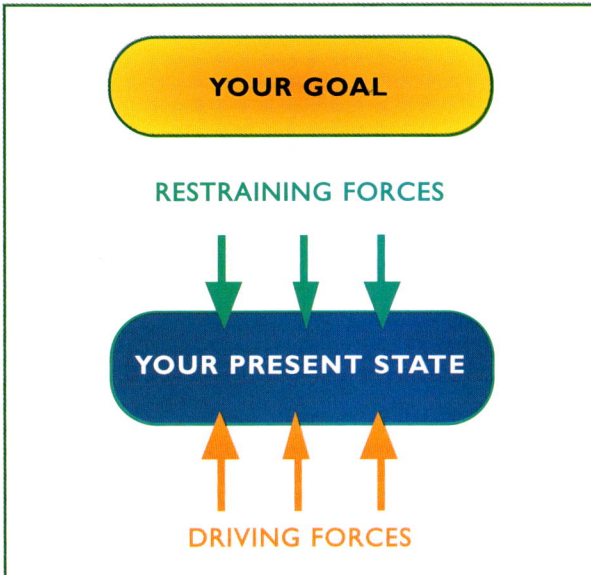

Copy the above diagram onto a blank page leaving spaces for your reflections. Fill in your dream or goal from **Exercise 2.1**. Then describe your present state. You will have a good sense of this after completing your personal profile **Exercise 2.2.** The purpose of this exercise is to analyse the forces that are likely to affect your commitment. To help you identify the driving forces consider your motives for taking part in sport and your reasons for pursuing your goals. These motives can be intrinsic such as pride, ambition, enjoyment, and challenge. They can also be extrinsic for example, prestige, reward, or pressure from others. Write these in the space for driving forces. These are the forces that are going to push you from your present state toward your goal.

To truly understand commitment you need to look at the forces that act against you. These are referred to as restraining forces. They can be more powerful than the driving forces, so think carefully as you complete this part of the exercise. The restraining forces are usually a mixture of personal factors and outside influences. Personal factors include lack of self-belief, poor time-management, fear of failure, unhealthy habits. Outside factors could include work pressures, family commitments, poor support systems, and apathetic team-mates.

Below are two examples of a force field analysis. You will see that there are arrows of various sizes next to each force. The thicker the arrow, the stronger the force. When you have looked at these examples, take some time to complete your own analysis, giving some consideration to the strength of each force.

EXAMPLE **Golf**

GOAL

TO REDUCE MY GOLF HANDICAP TO **28** OR LESS

RESTRAINING FORCES

Poor time management   Smokes 20 daily   Never practises   Takes no other exercise

CURRENT STATE

Handicap 32   Inconsistent swing   Low fitness level   Concentration a problem

Favourite pastime   Good for business   Want to be as good as my friends

DRIVING FORCES

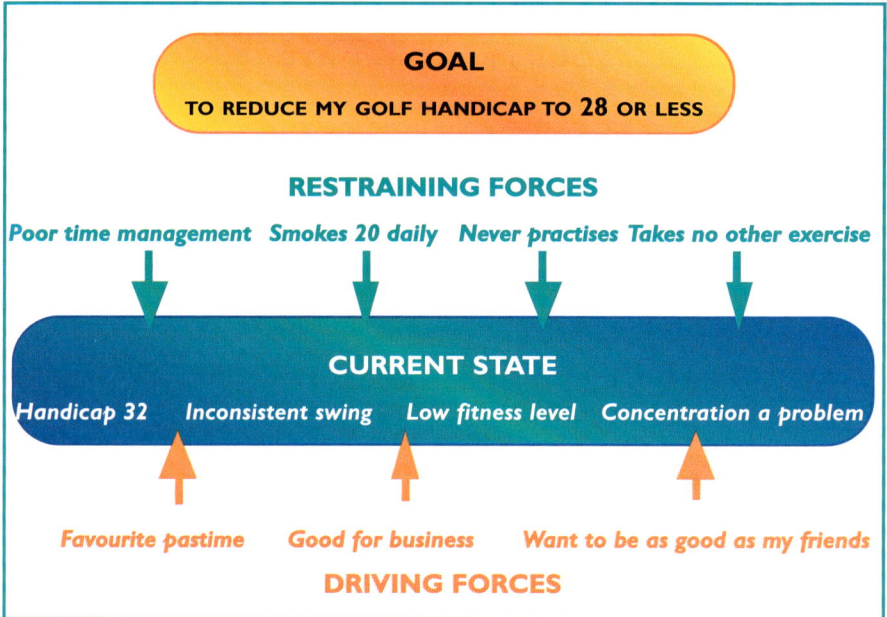

In this example it is clear that the restraining forces are very powerful. This person doesn't make time to practise, so she will have great difficulty in getting technically better. Her lack of fitness probably hampers her as she begins to tire over the last few holes. This will also affect her concentration. Even though she loves golf and wants to improve, she will have to work on her time management if she is to make progress. This extra time could be used to practise or get fitter, which will ultimately help her towards her goal.

EXAMPLE **Football**

GOAL
TO WIN PROMOTION TO DIVISION ONE

RESTRAINING FORCES

Defeatist attitude   *Low fitness levels*   *Poor organisation*   *No team spirit*

CURRENT STATE
DIVISION 2

New coach   *Challenge – the club has never played in division 1*   *A potential sponsorship deal*

DRIVING FORCES

In this example, there is a belief within the team that they are not good enough. This might stop some players giving full commitment. They are used to losing. When they lose a few games it confirms their self-doubt, so they train less. This leads to reduced fitness, poor organisation, and further defeats.

The new coach will have to work on breaking this cycle. He has the advantage of bringing new energy. If he is organised, players are more likely to respond positively. He can then create the challenge for them of playing in division 1. Sponsorship may be an incentive for some. This example shows how important factors outside of yourself can be, particularly in team sports. The external factors often need to be sorted out before players can bring all their energy into play for the betterment of the team.

In your analysis, pay particular attention to the restraining forces. These are the factors that drain energy, making less available for the pursuit of your sporting goal. Coaches will also find this exercise useful. It is helpful in trying to understand athletes who seem to have plenty of ability but lack commitment. There may be other factors in their lives that coaches are unaware of. If this exercise sheds light in this area, then coach and athlete can work together with greater understanding.

The last few exercises encouraged you to think about your commitment. The next section suggests ways of improving your commitment. At the beginning of the chapter, we described commitment as the engine that drives you toward your dreams. Having established where you want to go, where you are now and what it is going to take to get there, you must now start up the engine.

Setting targets or goals is a very effective way of guiding you on your journey. It gives you direction and a sense of achievement as each target is reached. Setting goals also directs and focuses your energy. It's difficult to stay motivated all the time. From time to time you get injured, you get tired, a winter storm keeps you indoors, you feel low or you feel like giving up. The player or athlete with short-term and long-term goals is more likely to survive such crises.

Passion allied to purpose can be an awesome combination

If you have no direction, you are likely to get bored, frustrated, or depressed. This undermines other aspects of your mental fitness, most notably your confidence. So setting goals is a very effective strategy to improve commitment.

On your marks – SET – GOAL!

Successful people commit themselves to reaching their goals or targets. Setting goals is a big step on the road to action. To get the best from goal-setting it is important to set appropriate goals. Goal-setting is a process and it is one of the key mental training strategies.

In **Exercise 2.1** you listed your dream and yearly goals. There are usually general in nature. They focus on a desire or outcome. They are called *general, long-term* or *outcome goals*. They serve as a starting point for your journey ahead. Setting goals based only on winning can affect motivation and self-confidence as losing may be equated with failure. It is helpful therefore to develop more *specific* or *short-term goals* which focus on improvements relative to your own standards. These are called *performance goals*. They focus on what you can do. The emphasis is on achieving certain measurable standards that are under your control.

The process of goal-setting helps you identify the steps that will take you closer to turning your dreams into reality. The guidelines overleaf will help you set performance goals. This is called SMARTER goal-setting.

DREAM GOAL

▽

YEARLY GOALS

▽

PERFORMANCE GOALS

▽

ACTION STEPS

Opposite: Ian McGeechan, 1997 British and Irish Lions rugby coach

Guidelines for **SMARTER** goalsetting

SPECIFIC

There are a number of ways to start this process. From your personal profile specify weaknesses to be worked on if your overall goal is to be achieved. For example, improve aspects of your fitness, develop particular skills, reduce anxiety before competitions. If your yearly goal is to take part in a particular event then specify the steps you will take in the lead-up to it.

MEASURABLE

This is easiest in sports where times or distances or points are recorded: for example, run 800 metres in under 2 minutes, score 9.2 for artistic impression, jump 1.9 metres. In team games you have to be more creative to come up with measurable goals other than scores: for example, reduce fouling by 25 percent, cross the gain line more often than the other team.

AGREED

You need to agree with yourself first that you are going to work towards your goals. It also helps to share your goals with a coach or other significant people. In team sports there will be team goals set between the coach and players. These should be agreed and communicated to the players at meetings. Within a team, players should have individual goals also.

REALISTIC

Goals should be achievable, with sufficient challenge in them to stretch you but not so difficult that you get discouraged if they can't be reached.

TIME FRAME

Put target dates on as many goals as possible. It doesn't mean they are set in stone. Obviously dates can be adjusted if necessary. It is usually best to put a date on the main goal and work back from that.

EXCITING

A goal that is worth striving for will keep your enthusiasm up until it is achieved. The secret then is to create new ones.

RECORDED

Write your goals because it commits you, gives you something definite to aim at, and allows you to make adjustments and review your progress.

You have identified your dream and yearly goals. Now you need to set some performance goals using the SMARTER guidelines as steps towards these goals.

_____

_____

_____

EXAMPLE: **Individual**

GENERAL GOAL | *to run a marathon*

SPECIFIC | *to run the New York marathon*

MEASURABLE | *complete it in under 3.5 hours*

AGREED | *arrange to train with running partner five days a week and tell others*

REALISTIC | *currently running in races up to 10k, need new challenge*

TIME FRAME | *four months to prepare, which is adequate*

EXCITING | *run for a charity to increase challenge*

RECORDED | *I will run the New York Marathon at the beginning of November in under 3.5 hours for a children's charity*

THE ACTION STEPS THAT FOLLOW FROM THIS
(put a date on each of these steps)

1. *Get a programme to ensure good direction.*
2. *Organise training times.*
3. *Buy appropriate shoes for training.*
4. *Contact a charity.*
5. *Send in entry form.*
6. *Arrange holidays, travel and accommodation.*

EXAMPLE: Gaelic football team

GENERAL GOAL   *to gain promotion to county league division I*

A coach meeting a team at the start of the season could begin with this general goal. To make it more performance-orientated he might start by analysing how many points are normally needed to gain promotion.

There are eight league matches, so the maximum points available are 16 (8 x 2). He estimates that 13, maybe 12, points will suffice to gain promotion. To achieve the requisite number of wins, he calculates they will have to score ten or more points in each game (and, obviously, concede fewer).

To achieve such scores will take a certain standard of fitness – the players will also have to improve their passing, tackling, and shooting. That will necessitate training three times per week.

So the team's goals are

1. *to amass at least 12 points in the league.*
2. *to score ten or more points in each game.*
3. *to concede fewer than ten points in each game.*

THE ACTION STEPS THAT FOLLOW
(put a date on each of these steps)

1. *Assessment of the team's current fitness.*
2. *Arrange training nights and times.*
3. *Players commit to attend two team training sessions per week.*
4. *Coach plans a training programme.*
5. *Players take responsibility for their lifestyle e.g reduce alcohol intake.*
6. *Video a match, analyse the video and then set more specific goals or benchmarks by which the players can analyse their own performances in each game.*

Goal-setting is effective only when it is followed by decisions and action. This is what separates winners from the rest. They are people of action. They commit.

If desire is your wishbone, then courage is your backbone. Your backbone gives you the get-up-and-go, the incentive to make any dream you dare to dream come true. It takes courage to excel, to be different from the crowd. There are risks but the rewards are great.

Courage

It takes courage to try to be
the very best you can be
when others around settle for mediocrity

It takes courage to sacrifice;
to work long, hard hours
when you could be relaxing

It takes courage to keep fighting when you're losing;
to seek out tough competition
when you know you'll probably be beaten

It takes courage to stick to your game plan
and the unrelenting pursuit of
your goal when you encounter obstacles

It takes courage to push yourself to places
that you have never been physically and mentally,
to test your limits, to break through barriers.

Risks

To laugh is to risk appearing the fool.
To weep is to risk appearing sentimental.
To reach out for another is to risk involvement.
To expose feelings is to risk exposing your true self.
To place your ideas, your dreams,
before a crowd is to risk their loss.
To love is to risk
not being loved in return.
To live is to risk dying.
To hope is to risk despair.
To try is to risk failure.

But risks must be taken, because
the greatest hazard in life
is to risk nothing.
The person who risks nothing,
does nothing,
has nothing, and is nothing.
They may avoid suffering and sorrow,
but they cannot learn,
feel, change, grow, love, live.
Chained by their attitudes,
they are a slave,
they have forfeited their freedom.
Only a person who risks is free.

IMPLICATIONS FOR COACHES

To get the best from yourself or those you coach takes time, energy, effort, dedication and consistency. All of these can be summed up under commitment. The exercises outlined so far can be used by coaches with individual athletes or teams. They give you a clear picture of what your athletes or players want to achieve and what they have to do to make their dreams a reality. As a coach you will appreciate that to be successful in sport, or indeed any other endeavour, you need to:

(a) know where you want to go, (b) assess where you are now, (c) know what it is going to take to get you there, and (d) commit yourself fully.

Before you, the coach, ask these questions of sportspeople under your care, you should be prepared to question yourself first. Being aware of your own motives, goals, values, and beliefs is vitally important. These will form the basis of your coaching philosophy. Your actions and behaviour will accurately reflect your underlying philosophy, and this will have a major impact on those you coach.

Ask yourself the key question: **Why do I coach?**
You need to take time to consider this question, because it is fundamental to developing those you coach. Here are some of the reasons people coach. Clearly, some of them are unhealthy. But often coaches are unaware of their real motives – and even when confronted with reality, they may not readily admit to them.

To win
To help people develop to their potential
To enhance ego
To gain power and control
To stay involved in sport
To satisfy a competitive urge
For fun and enjoyment
For financial gain

Coaching is a big responsibility, and you are in a very influential position, particularly if you coach juveniles. Your own commitment will be tested many times as your protégés lose form, get injured, drop out, ignore instructions, lose interest. In fact, your commitment will be tested even when they are doing well.

Opposite: Ron Harper of the Chicago Bulls

Coaches need to be aware that their philosophy, behaviours, and interactions are very influential in developing commitment. When the philosopher said, "It's very difficult to give away what you haven't got yourself", he could have been talking about commitment or indeed any other aspect of mental fitness.

Coaching is very often a public pursuit. It has been likened to swimming in a fishbowl – your every move is there for all to see and subject to testing on the field of competition. For this reason you need to be very clear about your coaching philosophy and your commitment to it. We all have a mental self-portrait – an image of ourselves as we would like to be and as we would like others to see us. This image is often unconscious, but we work hard to maintain it. Because coaching is such a public activity, the typical coach is constantly at risk of having that portrait damaged. A coach's actions and utterances are under public scrutiny, often by people who are subjective in their analysis. When the self-portrait is damaged or threatened, the coach usually takes protective steps. More often than not this is done unconsciously. But the resulting behaviour is witnessed by those closest to or working with that coach. For example, a coach may be criticised for using certain tactics but he may blame the players rather than the tactics.

The most common cause of conflict in a coach is a threat to his or her professional reputation or pride. He or she may have been saying things like "Enjoy the game", "Do your best", "It's the taking part that matters". But a series of poor performances by athlete or team could cause people to question his or her competence. The coach may then feel pressure to produce a winning performance resulting in instructions of a very different nature being given. Another cause of conflict is a discrepancy between the commitment of coach and performer. Coaches are often totally committed and get frustrated when they perceive apathy in players. A player's goals and reasons for involvement may be different to those of the coach.

So examining your coaching philosophy, approach to coaching and your own commitment as a coach as well as the commitment of the people you coach, is extremely worthwhile. All of the exercises in this chapter should also be undertaken by coaches. This process of reflection will help your coaching and ultimately those who you coach.

Opposite: Action from 1997 All-Ireland Ladies Gaelic Football Final

SUMMARY

Commitment is the effort and energy that goes into turning goals into reality. The intensity of one's commitment tends to be stronger when it comes from within although sport provides many external motives and rewards to complement this internal drive. Commitment is a vital ingredient in achieving success. It can be said of successful people:

they know where they want to go
they recognise where they are now
they understand what it is going to take to reach their goals
they commit themselves to getting there

Goal-setting is the primary strategy for directing effort and energy. You can start with general goals and draw-up more specific goals based on your personal profile.

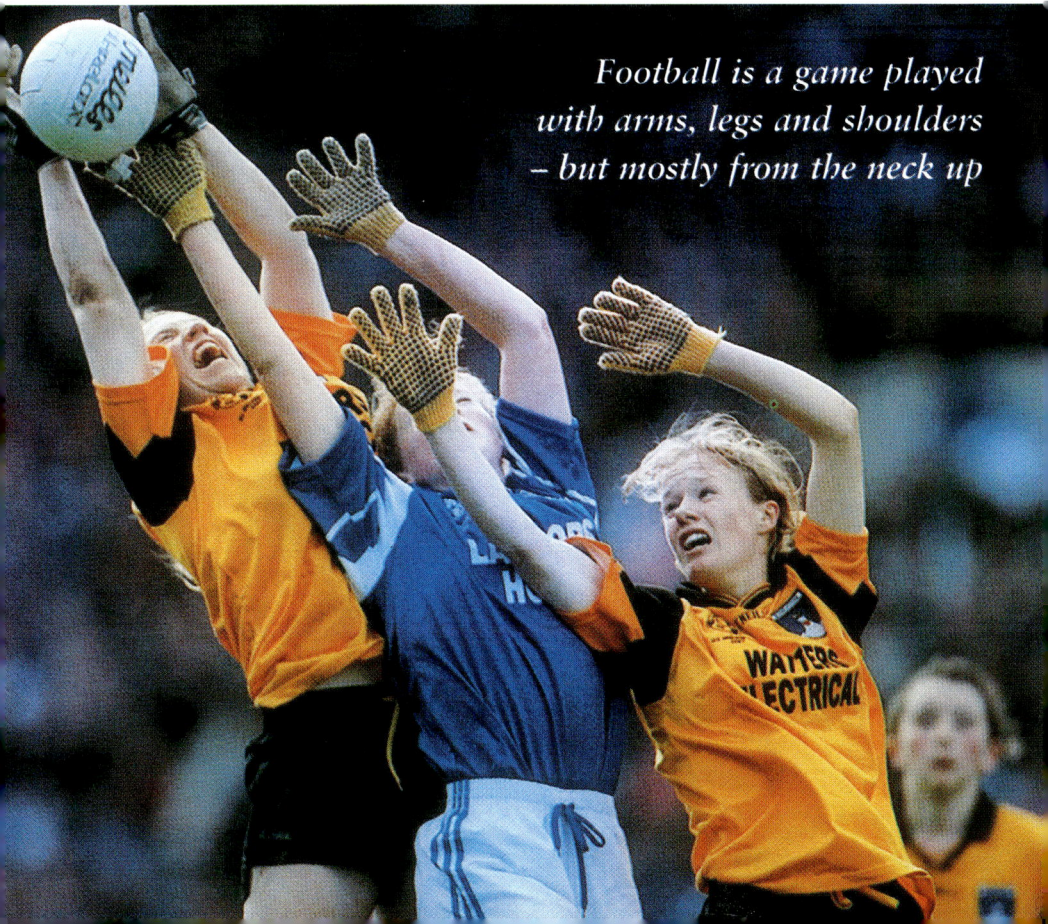

Football is a game played with arms, legs and shoulders – but mostly from the neck up

Winners are positive thinkers who see good in all things. From the ordinary they make the extraordinary

Chapter 3

BUILDING CONFIDENCE

WHAT IS CONFIDENCE?

HOW CONFIDENT ARE YOU?

STRATEGIES TO BUILD CONFIDENCE

IMPLICATIONS FOR COACHES

Opposite: Maurice Fitzgerald, 1997 gaelic footballer of the year

Life's battles don't always go
To the strongest or faster man,
But sooner or later
the man who wins
Is the man who thinks he can

*"I volunteered to take the penalty because
I felt pretty confident about scoring."*
(David O Leary, scorer of the winning penalty for Ireland
against Romania in the 1990 World Cup.)

*"I had the hardest year of boxing I ever had in 1991. But I've come back
stronger. In Barcelona, I honestly believe I might just sneak a little medal."*
(Michael Carruth, four months before winning his Olympic gold medal.)

Confidence is a state of mind that comes from knowing you have the abilities or resources to meet the demands of situations you are likely to face. It is also the belief that you can acquire the necessary competencies to reach your goals.

When you are confident you feel positive, optimistic, and in control – you expect to perform well. Low confidence is characterised by pessimism, doubt, anxiety, even dread. You expect to make errors, and when you do it confirms your doubts.

Expectations have a huge impact on performance. Seldom do people exceed their expectations. In a sense you set the scene with your thoughts, feelings, and attitudes. All of these are closely linked to your beliefs. Confidence is not something you are born with; it is learned; it develops throughout your life; it is largely based on the experiences you have had. In a sporting context your confidence is influenced by your interpretation of various things: the successes you have experienced; the setbacks you have suffered; feedback from significant people such as parents, teachers and friends, and the amount and type of preparation you have undertaken.

Confidence stems from the anticipation that you will perform well. Your expectancy becomes what is known as a self-fulfiling prophecy. The poem *You are what you think you are* summarises very well the nature of self-fulfiling prophecies.

Opposite: Michael Carruth

You are what you think you are

If you think you are beaten you are,
You think you dare not you don't,
If you like to win but think you can't
It's almost certain you won't.

If you think you'll lose you have lost,
For out in the world we find
Success begins with a person's will,
It's all in the state of mind.

If you think you are outclassed you are,
You've got to think high to rise,
You've got to be sure of yourself
Before you can win a prize.

Life's battles don't always go
To the strongest or faster man,
But sooner or later the man who wins
Is the man who thinks he can.

An essential ingredient in developing confidence is learning from mistakes. If sportspeople can practise in an encouraging atmosphere where mistakes are viewed as learning opportunities and feedback is encouraging they are more likely to be confident. On the other hand, if they are constantly criticised for their mistakes they take few risks in order to avoid censure and the opportunities to build confidence are lost.

It is vital to recognise that confidence is not a steady state. It can change throughout a season, from day to day, from hour to hour, even within a training session or competition. In order to truly understand confidence it is essential to look a little deeper and examine your belief system.

Identify your beliefs

Beliefs often create a self-fulfiling prophecy. This means that expecting something to happen actually contributes to making it happen. If many of your sporting beliefs are positive you are more likely to be confident about your ability. Unfortunately for many people their beliefs are disempowering and they create negative self-fulfiling prophecies which undermine confidence.

Take a few minutes to consider some general beliefs about sport and how these can influence people's confidence. Here are some common beliefs:

> "There's a prime age when you are at your best – it's all downhill after that."
> "That team cannot perform in wet weather."
> "A division 4 team does not have the resources to beat a division 1 team."
> "That track is fast – you'll run a good time on it."
> "Teams play better at their home venue."
> "You have to train abroad to be successful."

Because many beliefs are limiting, it is beneficial to identify and examine your own beliefs before you can build lasting self-confidence. Draw a line down the middle of a blank page. On one side write down your positive or empowering beliefs. These will be sentences that begin "I can" and "I will". On the other side write down your negative or disempowering beliefs. These will usually begin "I can't", "I don't have", "I'm not good at", "I find it impossible to".

The two examples below illustrate how beliefs can play a crucial role in the approach to competition.

American golfer Paul Goydos relates a story that shows the contrasting nature of beliefs even among professionals. Goydos, a seasoned player on the circuit was having dinner with Tom Watson, winner of numerous Majors. He had listened intently as Watson told stories about US Opens, British Opens, and Masters past. On leaving the restaurant Goydos realised a major difference between Watson and himself.

> *"He dreams about winning another Major;*
> *I just dream about playing in one."*

In 1989 as the English soccer season drew to a close, the destination of the league title hinged on the last match. Arsenal had to travel to Liverpool and win by at least two goals to become champions. The general belief was that it was difficult to beat Liverpool at Anfield but by two goals – that was almost impossible. To make matters worse Arsenal had never won by this margin at Anfield. Would Arsenal have the belief to overcome history and the confidence to play the type of attacking game that would be necessary to win by this margin? Following a 2-0 victory, Arsenal were crowned English League Champions for 1989.

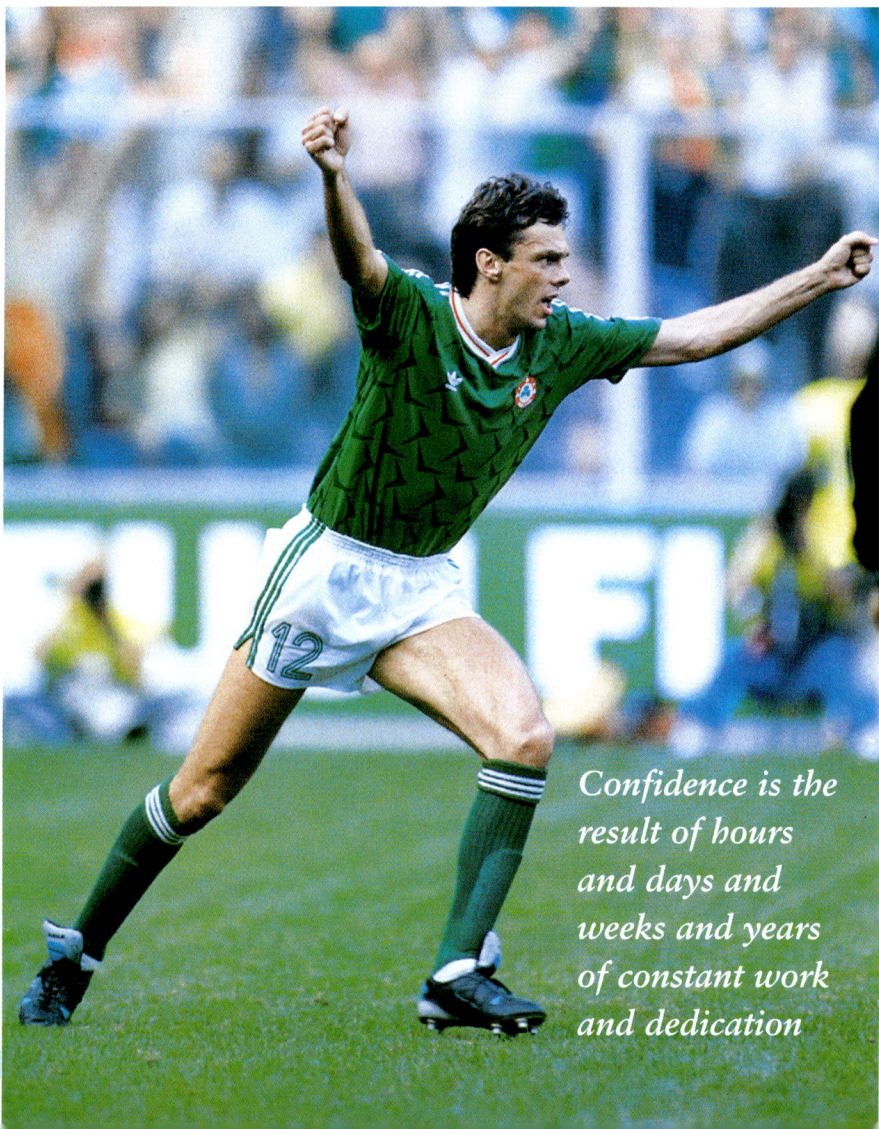

Confidence is the result of hours and days and weeks and years of constant work and dedication

HOW CONFIDENT ARE YOU?

Confidence is difficult to assess because it is ever changing. You can be confident for an event one week but a week later be lacking in confidence for a similar event – because the weather has changed, the venue is different, or the opposition is tougher. Confidence even fluctuates during a competition. Comparing yourself with the list of characteristics of confident and less confident competitors will give you a good indication of your confidence rating.

EXERCISE 3.2 **How do you compare?**

CONFIDENT COMPETITORS

1.   Believe they have the fitness, skills, and ability to perform well in given situations.
2.   Stick to the task even in adversity.
3.   Have a positive approach to training and competition.
4.   Take responsibility for their efforts and decisions.
5.   Challenge themselves to reach their targets, which are usually realistic.

LESS CONFIDENT COMPETITORS

1.   Have doubts about some or all aspects of their ability to compete adequately.
2.   Give up easily and appear to lose interest, especially in adversity.
3.   Think and speak negatively.
4.   Avoid responsibility by making excuses or blaming factors outside their control.
5.   Do not challenge themselves. Attempt either impossible tasks (which lead inevitably to failure and thus confirm doubts) or easy tasks (which allow success with minimal challenge and effort).

This exercise can also be used after competitions to assess the role of confidence as a factor in your performance.

Opposite: David O'Leary former Arsenal and Republic of Ireland player

Before getting into specific strategies, it is worth understanding a little bit about how the mind operates. Sit back and close your eyes for a few minutes and notice how many thoughts come and go. Now recall the last time you felt nervous or excited. Where do these thoughts and feelings originate? And how do they affect behaviour?

The mind has been likened to an iceberg. Most of the information, memories, images, and beliefs you have accumulated throughout your life are stored and processed beneath the surface, in the unconscious.

The unconscious is the most powerful part of your mind. From it many of your thoughts, feelings, attitudes, and behaviours originate. For the most part, you are unaware of the powerful influence the unconscious exerts. You generally become aware of your thoughts and feelings only when they come to the surface – in other words, when they enter consciousness.

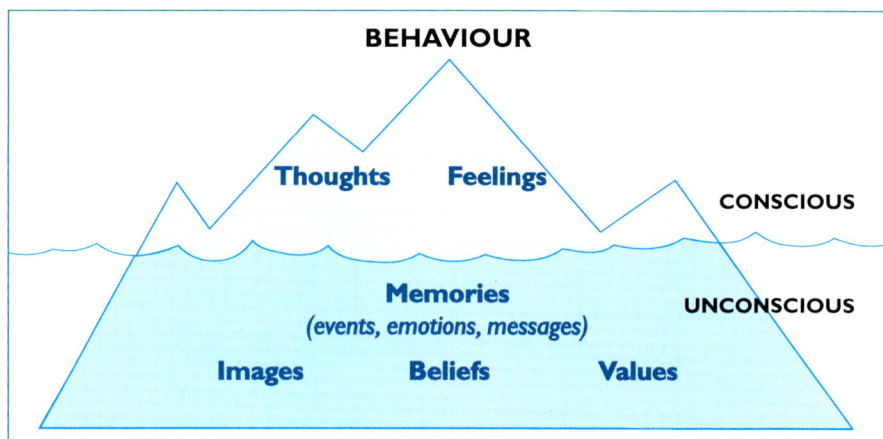

The diagram of the iceberg is a simple representation of the relationship between your inner world and your outer behaviour. It is a two-way channel. Most thoughts and feelings originate in the unconscious. These influence the way you behave. So if you exert some control over this process, you are likely to have thoughts that assist you rather than thoughts that disable or sabotage you. That is why looking at your beliefs is so important.

So how did your beliefs get there? You receive messages throughout your life. These messages come in many forms – remarks, gestures, opinions of others, and your interpretation of events that you experience. These messages are planted in your unconscious. All too often they are negative, limiting, and flawed. So becoming aware of the messages you have stored is essential to building confidence.

EXERCISE 3.3 Re-examine your beliefs

Go back to **Exercise 3.1** and examine your negative thoughts and beliefs. Take each belief in turn and consider how it was first planted in your mind. Remember, all beliefs are learned. Was it a remark by your parents, a coach, teachers, friends, or something you read in the paper? Maybe it was a generally held belief – but the fact that everyone believes something doesn't make it true. Re-examine these beliefs because too often they are inaccurate and you may not be aware of how much they affect your confidence.

In the forties and early fifties, running a mile in under four minutes was one of the great challenges in sport. Many runners were chasing the dream. Great athletes tried and failed. For ten years, they were coming within a second of the goal. Commentators said it was impossible – and the belief that it was impossible became widely accepted. One man who rejected popular superstition was Roger Bannister. He trained specifically for the challenge – and in 1954 ran 3 minutes 59.4 seconds.

Within two years of Bannister's breaking the barrier, most elite milers were running under four minutes. Their beliefs about the event had changed.

The breaking of the four minute mile barrier was a classic example of overturning a limiting belief. In 1994 Eamonn Coghlan became the first masters runner to run a sub four minute mile. It was interesting to see history repeated. Experts said it couldn't be done – great athletes had tried it and broken down – middle-aged tissues and joints would not take the training.

Actually, Coghlan didn't achieve his goal as a 40-year-old – he got injured. That of course was an opportunity for the doubters to say that if he couldn't do it at 40 he certainly had no chance of doing it at 41. To his great credit, Eamonn did not let all those negative thoughts, opinions, remarks, and words enter his unconscious. He filtered them out, and at 41 years of age he did what Bannister did – he acted out his self-fulfiling prophecy:

"It can be done and I can do it."

Since you are the one who learned your beliefs, you can readjust them and remove them if necessary. Your beliefs are deeply rooted and long-standing, and you have to constantly challenge them. The first step is to become more aware of your beliefs. To help increase your awareness select small segments of time and monitor thoughts that reflect your beliefs. Write down the relevant thoughts and any associated feelings. Gradually extend the period of monitoring. You can start at a few minutes and work up to a day.

Now that you are aware of their powerful influence, be ready to challenge your beliefs more often.

Where did this belief come from?

How is it affecting me?

How can I change it?

Do I want to store this information in my mind?

Is it likely to help or hinder me in the future?

Think of your beliefs as old tape recordings. If they are hindering you or holding you back wipe them out. The next exercise will help you record new messages and so begin the process of building confidence.

EXERCISE 3.4 Self-talk

Self-talk is a term used to describe our internal dialogue. We constantly react to situations, interpret events and act out our beliefs. Self-talk is the thoughts we experience and the comments we make to ourselves as these happen. Self-talk that motivates, affirms, and encourages is generally called positive self-talk. Negative self-talk tends to be critical, demeaning and disabling. Negative self-talk has been described as the opponent within and is often much more formidable than any individual or team we are likely to face. Here are some examples of self-talk:

Situation	Negative self-talk	Positive self-talk
A tennis player serves a double fault at a crucial juncture in the final set	*I've blown it. How could I be so stupid? Why didn't I serve for safety? I'm definitely in trouble now.*	*I'm playing well. I'm hitting the ball well. Relax and focus on this service. I have a good service.*
An injury means missing two months in the middle of the season	*I will miss the season. I never have any luck. I will lose all my fitness and everybody will get better than me. I will never be right again.*	*These setbacks occur in sport. I will work on other aspects of fitness that I never have time for. I will learn more about mental fitness and practise some mental training techniques*

Now think of situations in your sport and how you typically respond. This exercise is similar to the previous one in that it is helping you become more aware of the underlying factors that can affect your confidence. Consider both training and competitive situations when analysing your self-talk. What you should remember is that we all encounter similar situations, but it is how we react to them that accounts for many of the differences between us.

Shakespeare understood this well:

"There is nothing either good or bad, but thinking makes it so."

Self-talk can be practised so that your thoughts become encouraging, helpful, and positive for the most part. While talking positively to yourself will not automatically guarantee a better performance – negative self-talk will almost certainly undermine your confidence and take from your performance. If you allow negative or destructive thoughts to go unchecked they affect you in one or two ways. They influence your behaviour or attitude there and then and/or they become planted in your unconscious. When they go into the unconscious they further intensify your disempowering beliefs. Thus you have a vicious circle.

What can be done to change this?

Examining your beliefs and becoming more aware of the influences of your disempowering beliefs is an important starting point. A willingness to challenge these beliefs is the next step. To help you challenge your disempowering beliefs and develop self-talk that is confidence building, three strategies are outlined on the following pages.

EXERCISE 3.5 Thought stopping

You cannot stop thinking – but you can exercise some control over your thoughts. That's the purpose of thought stopping. You need to stop negative, destructive, and disempowering thoughts if you are to build confidence. If you allow these thoughts to linger, they undermine your confidence. So the idea is to stop them before they hurt your performance.

Thought stopping is a skill. That means you need to practise it regularly to become proficient at it. Like most skills, it will feel awkward at first, but when you start to see improvement you will be encouraged to practise more.

As you train and compete, be aware of your self-talk. When you catch yourself thinking negatively, use what is known as a cue to stop that type of thought. Cues might be shouting *Stop!* to yourself or clicking your fingers or slapping your thigh. Remember, negative self-talk is a habit and as such will be difficult to eradicate. For that reason work on thought stopping during training, when the pressure is light. When you get better at it in training, use it during low key events. Gradually it will become part of your routine. That doesn't mean negative thoughts will disappear entirely. It means that even though they will always come and go, you are not letting them control you.

We see examples of this on a regular basis. In interviews with successful individuals and teams after a close match where they appear to be beaten but claw their way to win, they often speak about staying focused on the job at hand even though thoughts of defeat flicker through their minds. Vincent Hogan in the book *Heroes of Irish Sporting Life* captured this brilliantly in an interview with Eamonn Coghlan on his return to the track in Madison Square Garden in 1993 for the masters mile after three years of retirement.

> *"With his first steps on Friday evening, Coghlan came to understand the magnitude of his new gamble. Word went around that the Mayor of Boston had skipped dinner with Bill Clinton so he could see Eamonn charge for glory. Within two laps, the arena was licked by flames of apprehension. Frank Conway, the so-called rabbit, went too quickly and only Wilson Waigwa had the speed to follow. Coghlan lost 30 yards on them in the first 300. He could feel the air grow thin.*
>
> *'I definitely wasn't comfortable,' he would observe. 'The wood was sinking from under me, leaving my legs lifeless. All I could think of was how I had set myself up for this. I mean, here we were standing for the Irish national anthem just minutes earlier and now I was virtually being tailed off after two laps. I could feel a sense of panic.'*
>
> *But the split times assured him that Waigwa's legs could not sustain the madness. The Kenyan's best time as a masters athlete was 4 mins 13 secs. Coghlan employed an old trick of forcing himself into something of a trance.*
>
> *'I call it just keying into the computer. I knew Wilson would come back to me. The important thing was to block out the negative thoughts.'*
>
> *At the mid-point it was clear that Coghlan was recovering. All eyes left Waigwa for the clock with two laps remaining as Coghlan thundered past. He crossed the line in 4.05 and the dome ceiling was almost blown into the Hudson River."*

Note how Coghlan changed the negative thoughts as they surfaced. We tend to think that successful sportspeople do not get negative thoughts. They do but they have learned to push them aside.

It can be done and I can do it

If you look at a painting in a cheap, unattractive frame you may easily disregard it. Yet the same painting in a more becoming frame can compel your admiration. This concept can be applied to self-talk.

Now that you are monitoring your thoughts carefully, it is time to develop the skill of reframing. This entails replacing negative thoughts with realistic or positive thoughts – reframe them. Below are some examples of negative thoughts and reframed alternatives.

NEGATIVE THOUGHTS	POSITIVE THOUGHTS
This is impossible	**This is a challenge**
I have to stop	**I'm tough and I can get through this**
I feel terrible	**My body is getting ready to perform**
This feels stupid	**This is a new skill so take it one step at a time**
I have to get this point	**Keep your eye on the ball and swing easy**
Push harder	**Relax – trust the body – I can do this**

Using some of your own negative self-talk statements from **Exercise 3.4** try reframing them into more positive statements. It is useful to consider a motivational statement ("I can do this" or "I love the challenge") or an instructional statement ("eyes on the ball") when you are reframing. For thought stopping and reframing to be effective you need to keep practising them until they become second nature. This is one skill that successful people have developed often unknown to themselves. They think everybody does this. To them it is common sense. This is how winners think. Now you can start to develop a winning

Opposite: Eamonn Coghlan, winning the World Championships 1983

habit, but it takes practice. Begin by practising thought stopping and reframing for short periods such as during the warm-up. Gradually extend the time so that a positive mindset can be maintained for the duration of a full training session.

EXERCISE 3.7 Affirm yourself

Another feature of confident performers is that their opinions about themselves are generally positive and optimistic. These self-suggestions are called affirmations.

From everything you have read so far it should be obvious that suggestions have a very powerful affect on your mind. Norman Vincent Peale in his famous book the *Power of Positive Thinking* has this to say about affirmations:

> *"If you or I or anybody thinks constantly of the forces that seem to be against us, we will build them up into a power far beyond that which is justified. But if, on the contrary, you mentally visualise and affirm and reaffirm your assets and keep your thoughts on them, emphasising them to the fullest extent, you will rise out of any difficulty regardless of what it may be."*

When is the last time you were praised, rewarded, or affirmed in a positive way? It doesn't happen too often for the majority of people. Rather than wait around, you can start affirming yourself. This can really feel silly when you start out, but you have everything to gain from it and nothing to lose. For self-affirmations to be effective, here are some guidelines:

Use the word "I".

Use positive phrases "I can", "I am powerful", "I have talent".

Use the present tense "I am calm and I can do this".

Use reminders like photographs, inspirational cards, or an image that reminds you of your affirmations.

Affirm yourself during the day, when you are going training and as you prepare for a competition.

Affirmations are even more powerful when they get into the unconscious. You can plant some of these affirmations in your own unconscious. If you repeat a couple of affirmations to yourself just before you go to sleep or glance at a visual reminder, then you have sown a seed that may germinate as you sleep.

It is vital to point out that positive thinking on its own does not build confidence.

> *"You can't just wake up one day and think you're good*
> *– you have to become good."*
> (Howard Ferguson, coach and author.)

The exercises outlined in this chapter are a small part of the overall preparation. The hours of hard work in training, developing fitness, skills, and tactical awareness are what really build confidence. Confidence grows with competence.

> *"The harder I work the more confident I feel."*
> (Michael Jordan, basketballer.)

Stepping into the competitive arena with the knowledge that you have prepared to the best of your ability is the foundation on which confidence grows. These strategies to build confidence are useful only if they are combined with effective training and practice. The following are some guidelines for effective training.

PRACTISE WITH PURPOSE

The idea behind training is to prepare to meet the demands of the competitions you are going to take part in. Training should provide opportunities for you to develop physical fitness, skills, tactics, and mental fitness. Train at competitive pace, train with purpose, and set up competitive situations in practice. It is not possible to be confident if you are not also competent.

ENSURE SUCCESS

Experiencing success builds confidence. At practice set up situations where you get it right. Sometimes you need to enter competitions where you know you will do well. This can give you a boost.

PLAN

When you see your training and competition programme planned out and there is method in your approach, you are more likely to feel confident about what you are doing. Disorganisation, haphazard training, no guidelines, and no forward planning undermine your confidence.

TRAINING PARTNER

Try and train with people who are positive and who challenge you. First of all, your coach should be encouraging, knowledgeable, organised, and challenging. If he or she isn't then think strongly about a change of coach. The people you train with can also affect your confidence. If they are negative, not serious about training, are of much lower ability than you, then you may not benefit to any great degree. Care should be taken if training with people who are much superior to you. You can easily lose confidence when you continually compare yourself to them.

LOOK AND ACT CONFIDENT

Sometimes people have doubts when they see how confident their opponents look and act. The clothes they wear, the equipment they have, and the easy way they walk and talk. Turn this to your advantage by always looking and acting as confidently as you can, particularly at competitions. If you have a tendency to think negatively when you see your opponents, your body language will betray your thoughts, so great care is needed. As you are practising reframing, be aware of acting confidently also.

Journalist Paul Kimmage of *The Sunday Independent* described this very well in an article on Formula 1 driver Michael Schumacher.

> *"There is something about his body language as he steps from his car this morning, something about his arrogant strut as he crosses the tarmac . . .*
> *It's his chin. The thing that strikes you most is the way he carries his chin. High. Imperious. Godly. It's a chin that says 'my name is Michael Schumacher and I'm the best driver in the world'."*

Opposite: Michael Schumacher

*It's a chin that says
'my name is
Michael Schumacher
and I'm the best
driver in the world'*

IMPLICATIONS FOR COACHES

A coach is one of the most influential people in a player's or athlete's sporting life. In addition to planning the fitness programme, setting up skills practice, and developing tactical awareness, coaches need to realise that much of what they do and say impacts on their performers' mental fitness especially confidence.

Reflect for a moment on what you do and say in your coaching role. Consider how this impacts on the people you coach.

FEEDBACK

What do you say when you are giving feedback? (Praise or criticism).
Think about the actual language you use.

How do you give feedback?
The focus here is more on the way you say things i.e. how emotional you are, what is your body language like?

When do you give feedback about competition?
Do you give it immediately after the event, the same evening, a few days later, or do you talk about it at all?

When do you give feedback in training?
Is it when you see something performed correctly or incorrectly, to the whole group, to each individual, at the beginning, or when training is over?

What's your philosophy on feedback?
Do you highlight mistakes and tell people how it should be done or do you ask them what they think happened? Do you praise liberally or do you think praise will go to their head and use it very sparingly?

SETBACKS

How do you help your performers cope with disappointment?
How do you build their confidence when they are performing poorly?
What type of support do you provide when they are injured?

TEAM MATTERS

How do you create team spirit?
How do you make each member of a team feel important, especially substitutes?

PLANNING

Do you set goals with or for your performers?
How much planning do you put into your training programme?
Do you discuss training with them or do you tell them what to do?

There are no right or wrong answers to any of these questions. The purpose of asking them is to reinforce the point that the coaching process and coaches' actions have an impact on performers' confidence and behaviour. Coaches need to consider how their actions contribute or take away from their athletes' sporting performance. There are many good books on coaching that examine the areas of communication, feedback, planning, team-building, and a performer centered approach (see Appendix 1).

SUMMARY

Confidence is a state of mind that comes from knowing you have the abilities or resources to meet the demands of situations you are likely to face. It is also the belief that you can acquire the necessary competencies to reach your goals. When you are confident you expect to perform well. Many of your expectations stem from your beliefs. If your beliefs are negative or disempowering it is vital to become aware of how they undermine your confidence. Re-examining your beliefs, monitoring your internal dialogue (self-talk) and affirming yourself are some of the strategies that can be used to build your confidence. Confidence grows with competence and this is developed through regular and effective training as well as thorough preparation.

*People who enjoy what they are
doing invariably do it well*

Chapter 4

MAINTAINING CONTROL

WHAT IS CONTROL?

RATE YOUR CONTROL

STRATEGIES TO MAINTAIN CONTROL

IMPLICATIONS FOR COACHES

Opposite: Action from the 1997 All-Ireland Camogie Final

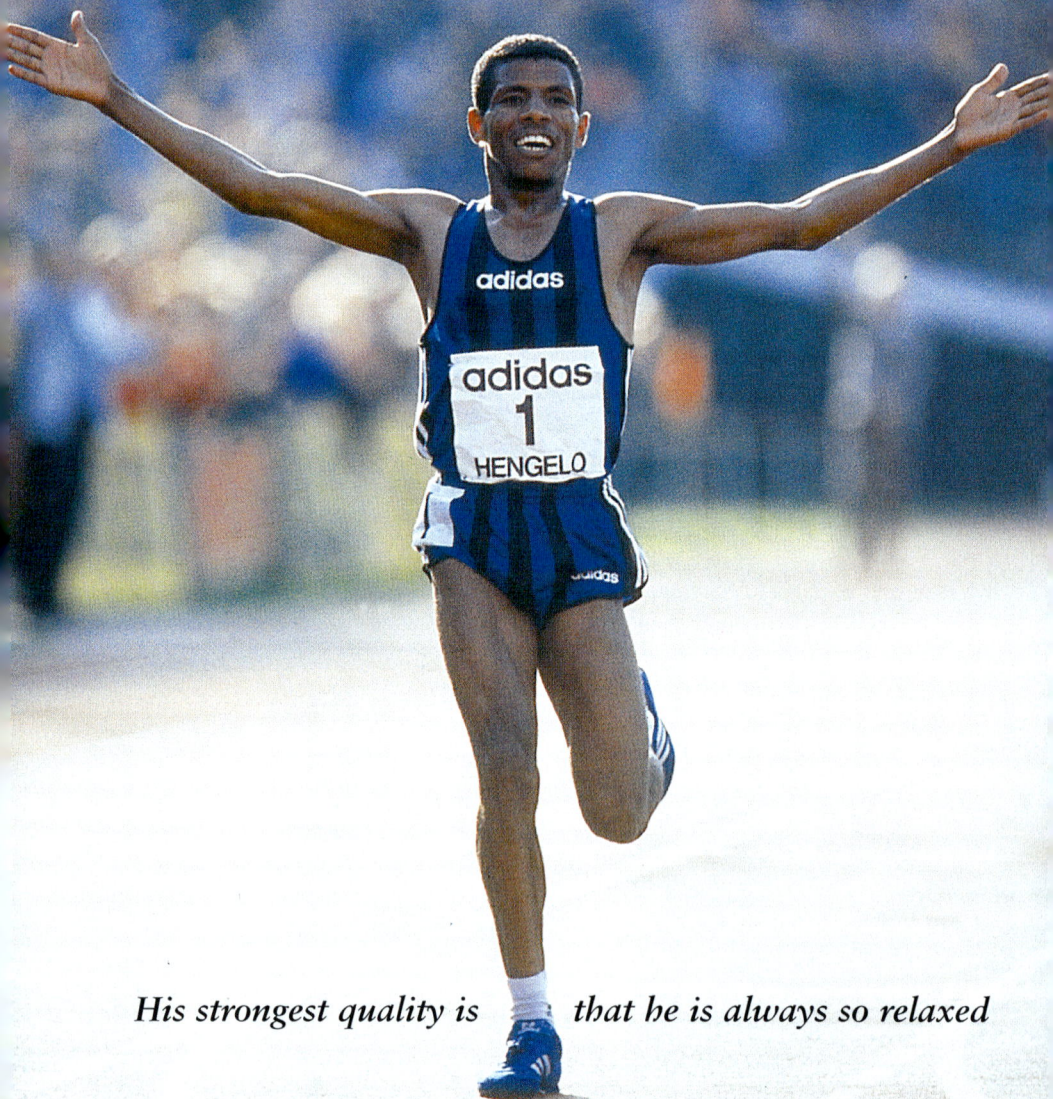

His strongest quality is   that he is always so relaxed

"His strongest quality is that he is always so relaxed. It amazes me that he seems immune to the pressure and stress that all athletes face. He respects his rivals, but fears no distance, no opponent."
(A description of Haile Gebrselassie, Olympic
and World champion at 10,000m by Jos Hermans.)

*"The worst thing of all was watching myself on television behaving very badly. My perceptions had been so distorted by rage that I hadn't actually remembered what had happened accurately. I was convinced I'd only kicked Nigel once, but that wasn't the case at all.
I was out of control"*
(Brian McClair, Manchester United, after a sending off.)

Sport by its nature stirs up a variety of thoughts and feelings. In the previous chapter many of the thoughts associated with sport were examined. Sport also triggers the whole range of emotions from joy, excitement, exhilaration and pride, to fear, frustration, anger, disappointment and depression. Thoughts and emotions have a profound effect on sporting performance because they are at the root of most of our actions and behaviour. Recognising this link and using this awareness to respond in appropriate ways is the essence of control. Control is also referred to as self-management or self-discipline. Like the other aspects of mental fitness, control is learned and therefore it can be developed through practice and experience. Learning to control your thoughts and emotions is essential to getting the best out of yourself, particularly in competitive situations. Of all the factors that influence how you perform in sport, your own internal environment is the one over which you can exert most control.

Failure to control thoughts and feelings has hindered many from realising their true potential. Negative thinking and emotions such as fear, anxiety, embarrassment and anger, erode self confidence, destroy concentration, and eventually weaken commitment. Not only do they affect your mental fitness, but they can diminish

---

Opposite: Haile Gebrselassie

your physical performance. A negative internal environment creates excessive stress and tension, which can express itself as muscle tightness, poor co-ordination, and motor skill impairment.

"Pressure creates tension, and when you're tense, you want to get your task over and done with as fast as possible. The more you hurry in golf, the worse you probably will play, which leads to even heavier pressure and greater tension."
(Jack Nicklaus, winner of 18 Majors.)

All pressure is self-inflicted; It comes from within

If your thoughts and feelings can be so influential then it is worth understanding a little about their impact on your sporting performance. A sporting event is a trigger to a range of thoughts and emotions. The same event will stir up a variety of reactions in each of the competitors taking part in it. How individuals perceive and interpret a sporting situation and the things that occur within it is the key to understanding their behaviour and actions. The extent to which a sportsperson can control this process will have a huge bearing on how he or she will perform. Leading up to an event and throughout it, the mind is constantly bombarded with a variety of stimuli. External stimuli include opponents, the event, your coach, the weather, the venue, team-mates, family and friends. Internal stimuli include your own thoughts, feelings, memories, beliefs and images. You know from the previous chapter that these internal stimuli can originate in the conscious or unconscious part of your mind.

In a sense it is not the stimuli that are important, because they are an integral part of sport, but your perception and interpretation of these stimuli. If you understand this process a little more it increases your chances of exercising control. Let us look at three examples before examining the underlying process.

- Mary is warming up when her opponent arrives. Mary's thoughts start to wander:

    "She looks so fit. Now I know why she is the champion for the last four years. Oh I hope I don't make a fool of myself."

    Mary starts to feel uptight and anxious.

- John wakes up the morning of an important event and just about makes it to the toilet. This will be the first of many visits over the next couple of hours. His stomach feels funny and he doesn't want to eat too much. He is thinking:

    "Here I go again. I'm all uptight and nervous and I never play well when I feel like this."

- The team travelling on the bus to the final seems relaxed. They have trained hard, they are well prepared, and they are confident in their ability. In the changing room everybody is upbeat and looking forward to getting out on the pitch. There is a pride and bond when they huddle together for the last time.

The mind perceives and interprets stimuli in two key ways. We have a rational or thinking mind and an emotional or feeling mind. They work in tandem. To help you understand their influence they have been separated here for clarity.

Opposite: Jack Nicklaus

RATIONAL MIND

The rational mind generates a series of thoughts based on what it sees in the present, with a strong influence from the unconscious also. These thoughts can trigger emotions. This mental activity then affects the type of behaviour or attitude we portray in response.

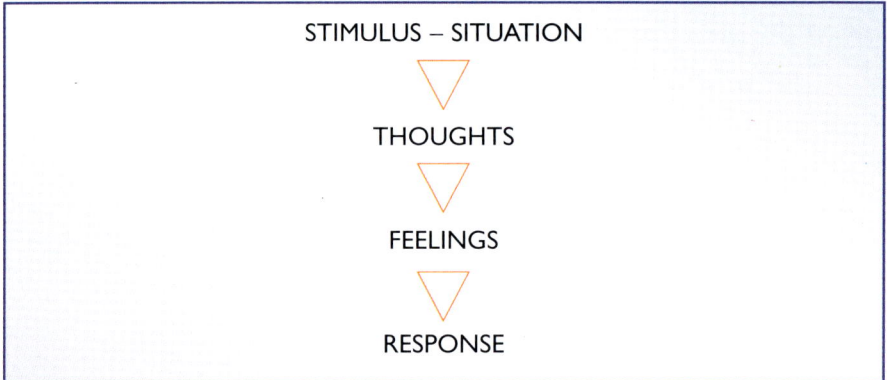

STIMULUS – SITUATION

▽

THOUGHTS

▽

FEELINGS

▽

RESPONSE

In the examples presented, Mary's case is typical of this process.

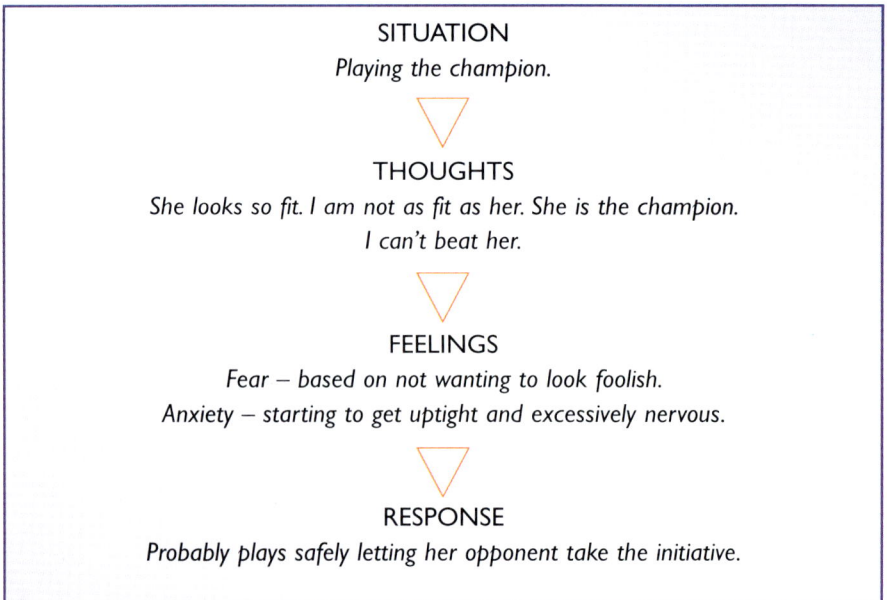

SITUATION
Playing the champion.

▽

THOUGHTS
She looks so fit. I am not as fit as her. She is the champion.
I can't beat her.

▽

FEELINGS
Fear – based on not wanting to look foolish.
Anxiety – starting to get uptight and excessively nervous.

▽

RESPONSE
Probably plays safely letting her opponent take the initiative.

Mary, with practice, could have a different approach to the same situation.

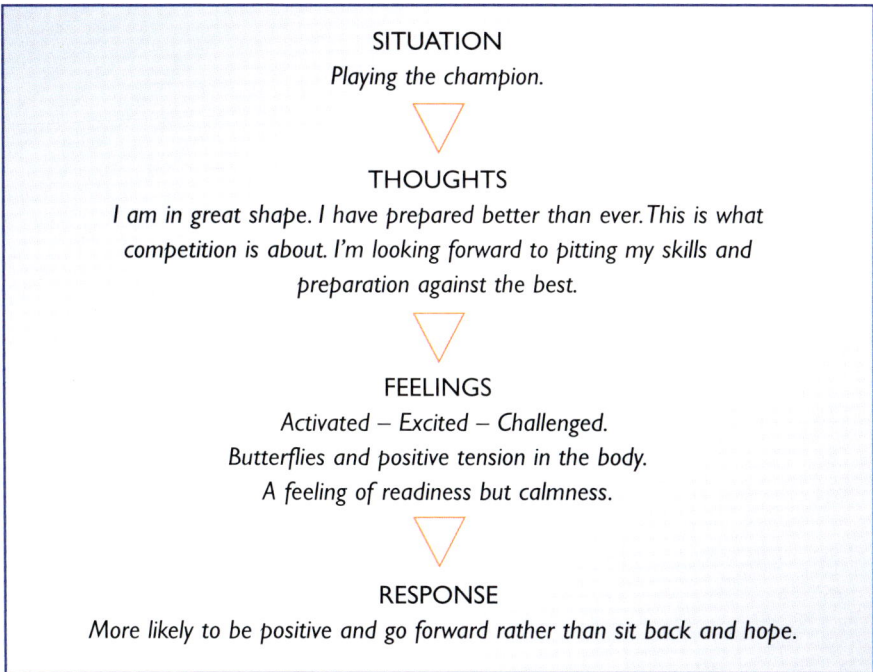

SITUATION
Playing the champion.

▽

THOUGHTS
I am in great shape. I have prepared better than ever. This is what competition is about. I'm looking forward to pitting my skills and preparation against the best.

▽

FEELINGS
Activated – Excited – Challenged.
Butterflies and positive tension in the body.
A feeling of readiness but calmness.

▽

RESPONSE
More likely to be positive and go forward rather than sit back and hope.

You can see from this example that the thoughts tend to start the process. So taking control of your thoughts can affect your approach and response to situations.

EMOTIONAL MIND

The next example shows that the mind also reacts emotionally to stimuli. We are not as aware when this is happening because the rational mind seems to be by-passed and the emotional mind is triggered directly.

```
                    STIMULUS – SITUATION
                              ▽
                         FEELINGS
                              ▽
                         THOUGHTS
                              ▽
                         RESPONSE
```

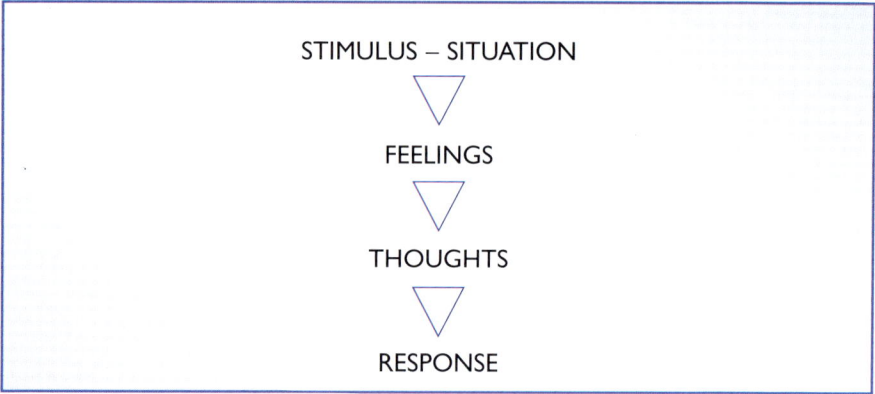

In this mode the feeling is experienced first – probably based on memory. In the example of John, the feelings are activated first. He is feeling very nervous and he begins to think negatively when he feels like that. He responds by getting more tense. In this state he is unlikely to play to the best of his ability.

On the other hand when he feels like that he could think about it differently.

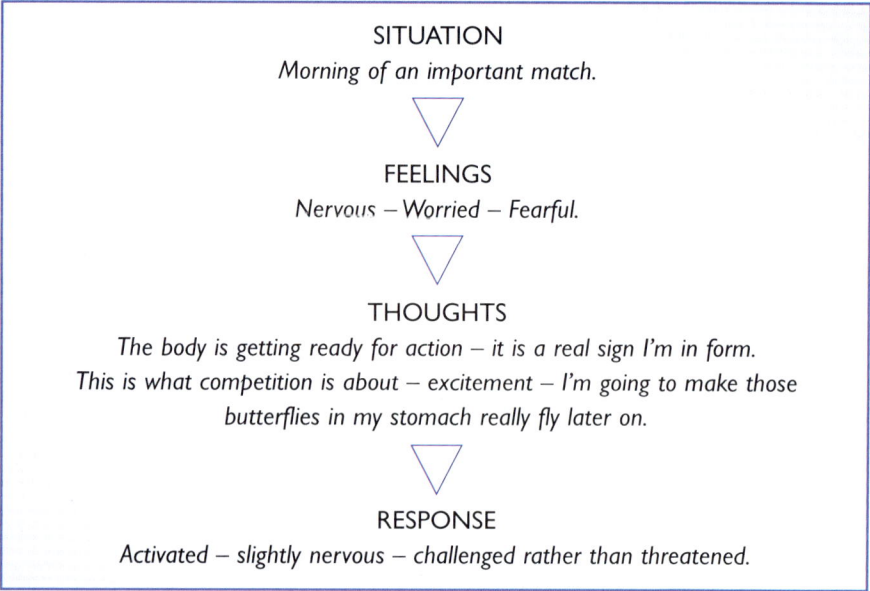

```
                        SITUATION
               Morning of an important match.
                              ▽
                         FEELINGS
                  Nervous – Worried – Fearful.
                              ▽
                         THOUGHTS
     The body is getting ready for action – it is a real sign I'm in form.
    This is what competition is about – excitement – I'm going to make those
                  butterflies in my stomach really fly later on.
                              ▽
                         RESPONSE
      Activated – slightly nervous – challenged rather than threatened.
```

This interpretation means John is more likely to play to his capabilities. Nerves on the morning of a competition are natural. The mind and body work as one and the reactions such as going to the toilet frequently are normal as the body readies itself for the rigours of competition. Unfortunately, many sportspeople don't realise this and regard the reactions as a negative sign.

RATIONAL AND EMOTIONAL MIND

In the team example a mixture of thoughts and emotions is being generated. This is often the case in sport. The important issue is not which comes first but taking control of your thoughts and feelings as soon as possible, especially when they are negative. If you do not control what is going on in your mind, then you are likely to be an inconsistent performer. How else can we explain the differences in performance from week to week? Physical fitness and skill do not change significantly in a week, unless you have overtrained or abused the body in some way. Most of the inconsistencies we see in sport are due to mental factors.

THE RELATIONSHIP BETWEEN MIND AND BODY

The thoughts and feelings we have not only influence our attitude and the way we behave, they also exert considerable influence on our physical responses. Emotions in particular have a direct effect on a multitude of physical reactions. This process can create an internal environment that is conducive to performing well or one that is responsible for a poor performance. How does this happen?

When a strong thought or feeling is being experienced other areas of the brain are activated. These include the hypothalamus, which initiates a series of hormonal responses, and the medulla, which activates the autonomic nervous system. The effects of this activation can be seen in the cardiovascular system, the muscles, the urinary system, the digestive system, and breathing.

Understanding that there is a direct link between the brain and the body is crucial to anybody involved in sport. This link is involuntary, meaning that many of the body's organs are stimulated automatically without us being aware that it is happening. This is not a problem when the stimulation leads to positive reactions and responses. But for many sportspeople when their minds become flooded with thoughts and emotions that are unhelpful, the signals that are then sent to the body hinder rather than enhance performance.

THE RELATIONSHIP BETWEEN MENTAL STATE AND ENERGY

POSITIVE MENTAL STATE

Thoughts	Emotions
I have the ability	Challenged
I am in great shape	Optimistic
I am confident	Excited

HIGH ENERGY – ACTIVATED

Full of energy, alert, light, in control,
slightly nervous, enthusiastic, positive

NEGATIVE MENTAL STATE

Thoughts	Emotions
I can't	Afraid
I'm not in shape	Frustrated
I'm not good enough	Tense

LOW ENERGY – STRESSED

Tense, drained, the body feels tired and heavy,
irritated, overwhelmed,
maybe apathetic or bored

This is simplified to give you a general idea of how your physical state is linked with your mental state. There are variations to the above. One obvious example is anger. When angered some people can be energised and charged up. Sometimes this can lead to a lift in performance. The pep talk to teams can be an example of this. This, however, is only a temporary state and can just as easily lead to a drop in performance, or behaviour that may lead to dismissal from the event.

So great care is needed when you are triggered to anger. Often anger is used to motivate sportspeople. The problem with this is that the response can be highly unpredictable. Creating an emotional state where you feel excited, challenged, or buzzed is better in the long term.

The tables showing the link between mental state and energy levels also give some indication of the powerful flow between body and mind. Consistent performers create a mental state that activates the body in a way that is going to enhance performance. Often they do this automatically. They have learned over the years what works for them. Unfortunately, many sportspeople have not learned to control their mental states, with the result that they perform below capability.

THOUGHTS

In the last chapter we looked at how messages are often limiting and negative. They continue to exert influence years later because the mind references many of its present thoughts against the information it has stored from the past. How often do we see lesser-known players lead big golf tournaments into the last day only to collapse as the bigger names loom up beside them on the scoreboard. Each year at Wimbledon we see unseeded players poised to win the final set against a big-named player only to lose in the end. You can be sure that their mental state is largely responsible for their collapse. At a deep level they don't believe they can win and even though they may be trying to talk positively to themselves their current thinking is not consistent with their deeper messages.

EMOTIONS

The unconscious mind also remembers feelings. Many of these feelings are associated with events and people. In his best-selling book *Emotional Intelligence*, Daniel Goleman describes this process:

> *"When some feature of an event seems similar to an emotionally
> charged memory from the past, the emotional mind responds
> by triggering the feelings that went with the remembered event.
> The emotional mind reacts to the present as though it were in the past."*

Emotions also have a powerful effect on sporting performance. Like thoughts, they have the power to drain the body of energy or create an inner tension that hinders good performance. Alternatively they can contribute to a state that promotes successful performances.

AROUSAL

Arousal is a general physiological and psychological state of activation. It ranges from flatness to over-arousal. Arousal level is a reflection of mental state. Performance tends to suffer when a person is in either a state of under or over-arousal

| FLATNESS | OVER-AROUSAL |

Each person has an optimal level of arousal associated with best performance. The important thing for sportspeople and coaches to note is what level of arousal works best for them. A certain amount of arousal and nervousness is normal and should be welcomed. Two feelings which tend to contribute to arousal level are anxiety and fear.

ANXIETY

Anxiety is an emotional state with feelings of nervousness, tension, worry and apprehension associated with over-arousal. Anxiety can refer to a personality trait or a changing mood state. There is a strong link between anxiety and performance. Anxiety usually has a negative effect on performance.

Symptoms of anxiety

Physical

Muscles tense-up producing a feeling of heaviness and tiredness.
Muscle tension also reduces flexibility and impairs skill.
Excessive sweating.
Dryness in the mouth.
Racing heart.
Feeling nauseous.
Going to the toilet frequently.

Mental

Mind racing.
Many negative thoughts.
Difficulty concentrating.
Impaired judgement.
Give up more easily.
Frustration.

These symptoms indicate why anxiety usually has a negative impact on performance. Experience eventually teaches some people how to deal with it, but too many sportspeople never come to terms with anxiety. One of the problems with anxiety is that it can occur when you least expect it. You could play well throughout a season and qualify for finals. On the day when you want to give your best, you get an attack of the jitters and you end up performing below par.

At the 1980 Moscow Olympics, Sebastian Coe was the red-hot favourite in the 800 metres. He had qualified smoothly for the final and his personal best was two seconds faster than his nearest rival. Coe finished second much to everyone's surprise but it was the ineptitude of his performance that stunned people. Here is how Coe described the lead-up to that final.

> *"I've never known pressure like it. I thought people had exaggerated, but they hadn't. There was no comparison. I'd felt pressure going into the Europa Cup final the year before, but it just wasn't the same thing. It began after the semi-final. I can remember looking down into my food at dinner amid the hubbub of the huge crowded restaurant, and glancing up and catching Peter's eye. He must have sensed I was uneasy because he smiled and said, 'Don't start now'. It was unusual for me, I'd never been like that so long before a race. I had the worst night's sleep I've ever had, just lying there listening to my own heartbeat, thinking to myself, you've coped with the pressure all the year, for heaven's sake take a grip! But it was the same next day. At lunch I knocked over my orange juice, and then dropped the cream carton into my cup of coffee. I suddenly felt ungainly, conscious of my own awkwardness. In the afternoon I couldn't sleep again, which is rare for me. Peter was up in the room, and he knew what was going on, but he knew that saying anything wouldn't help.*

I can remember the relief of getting on the move at last, going down to the stadium. But leaving the village my attitude was all wrong. I wanted to hurry into the warm-up, I didn't want to be alone. I'd already gone through the nervous bit, and now I was detached, disconnected. Mentally, I was an hour ahead of schedule. Normally, the detached phase happens in the few minutes before the race, when you've done the physical and mental wind-up and you're ready to cut out everything: voices, faces, sounds. But I was like this with forty-five minutes still to go. The race had that written all over it, it was a disinterested race, someone going through the motions."

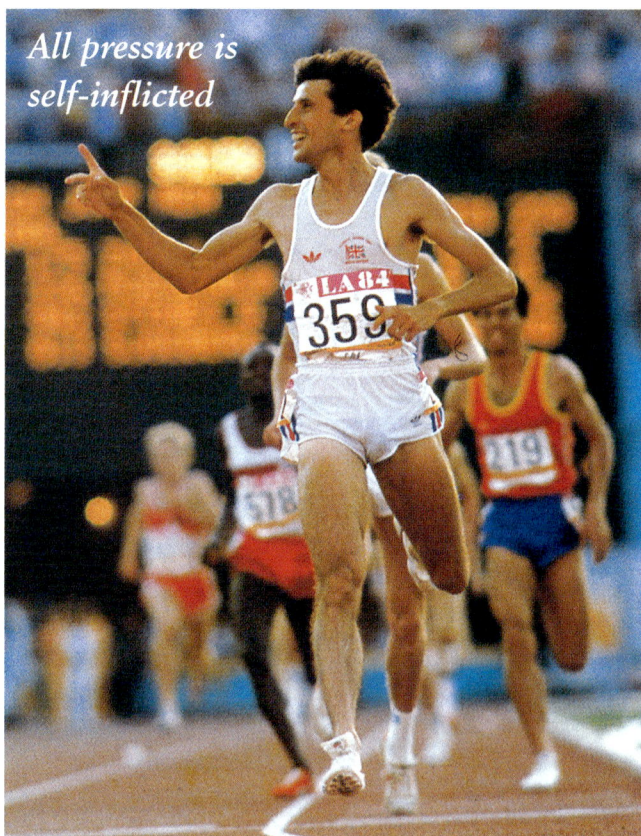

All pressure is self-inflicted

When this happens to someone a couple of times he or she becomes aware of how devastating anxiety can be to performing well. Unfortunately awareness alone does not offer a solution. Later in the chapter, you will find some strategies to regulate anxiety.

FEAR

Some people may associate fear with cowardice or the threat of injury. These are elements of fear, but the greatest fear in sport is the fear of failure. Why are so many people afraid to fail? Afraid to make the move that could be the winning of the event?

The answer probably lies in the threat to their self-esteem. Self-esteem is how you feel about yourself. The two important aspects of self-esteem are the beliefs that you are capable and that you are likeable. You can see how sport can be so threatening to these two beliefs. When you compete you are in a way putting yourself at risk. You are taking a social risk. You risk criticism, failure, embarrassment, and even ridicule. This can express itself in thoughts such as:

"What will other people think of me if I lose or screw up?"
"If I lose or make a mistake others will think I am no good."
"I don't want to let others down."

So instead of taking risks or making winning moves, many competitors play safe or make excuses. You hear competitors before events saying:

"I haven't trained as well as I would like but sure I'll give it a go."
"I never do well on this course."
"I'm not feeling well."

They are letting you know in advance that there is a reason in case they don't do well. Or you hear the excuses afterwards:

"I wasn't fully fit, I needed the game."
"I was out late last night."

These type of excuses deflect attention away from the performer to some outside source. The underlying fear is that if I make a mistake or don't play well, I won't be well liked or people will think I am not good enough.

Fear of failure leads to as much underachievement as anxiety does. Julie Heldman, a former tennis player, summarised the effects of this fear very well:

Opposite: Sebastian Coe winning the Olympic 1500m title 1984

*"Most tennis players don't play to win, they play not to lose.
When you play not to lose, you go out and do your best
but you don't go beyond that. You're not willing to put yourself
on the line and do everything in your power to win."*

The bottom line is that our fears about what other people think are imagined. In reality, most people are so preoccupied about themselves that they are not thinking about you.

DOING YOUR BEST

The central message in this book is that success is doing **your** best. It is only when you come to terms with this that you become a consistent performer. The most important person to please is yourself. When you develop this frame of mind you begin to take control.

Tom Watson read an excerpt from Theodore Roosevelt's famous *Man in the Arena* speech at the Ryder Cup dinner in 1993 that really captures the message: "Do your best and ignore the critics."

"It is not the critic who counts, not the one who points out how the strong man stumbled or how the doer of deeds might have done them better. The credit belongs to the man who is actually in the arena; whose face is marred with sweat and dust and blood; who strives valiantly; who errs and comes up short again and again; who knows the great enthusiasms, the great devotions and spends himself in a worthy cause and who, if he fails, at least while bearing greatly so that his place shall never be with those cold timid souls who know neither victory nor defeat."

Awareness of your state of mind and the ability to create thoughts and feelings that will help you perform better is the skill of self-control. As has been stated before, this ability is learned and improves with practice.

RATE YOUR CONTROL

EXERCISE 4.1 **Best performance**

Think of a recent competition where you performed at or close to your best.

1   What were your thoughts leading up to the event?

_____

2   How did you feel coming up to the event?

Worried (some doubts)	0	1	2	3	4	5	Confident (no doubts)
Extremely anxious	0	1	2	3	4	5	Competitive nerves
Flat	0	1	2	3	4	5	Activated
Pessimistic	0	1	2	3	4	5	Optimistic

3   How did you feel during the event?

Worried (some doubts)	0	1	2	3	4	5	Confident (no doubts)
Extremely anxious	0	1	2	3	4	5	Competitive nerves
Flat	0	1	2	3	4	5	Activated
Pessimistic	0	1	2	3	4	5	Optimistic

4   To what extent were you in control of your thoughts and feelings?

_____

EXERCISE 4.2 **Poor performance**

Repeat this exercise using a recent competition that you were dissatisfied with or where you performed poorly.

EXERCISE 4.3 **Taking control**

Reflect on the different states of mind on each occasion. Do you think you could have intervened at any stage before or during the poor performance? Identify where by answering the following questions.

1   How do you prepare mentally for a competition? Do you have a consistent routine? Do you take steps to get into the right frame of mind?

_____

_____

2   How do you react to situations that occur within an event? List some of the critical situations or incidents that are likely to happen and your typical response. If your response is likely to lead to playing poorly, what would be a more positive response?

_____

_____

3   How do you prepare mentally for a training session? Do you have a goal in mind? Can you turn a poor mental state around before you start or during training?

_____

_____

The strategies for maintaining control in the following pages and those to improve concentration from page 121 onwards are designed to help you create a mental state that is conducive to performing well consistently.

STRATEGIES TO MAINTAIN CONTROL

Now that you are aware of the powerful link between thoughts, emotions, and your performance, you can see the importance of trying to exert some control over them. You cannot prevent yourself from thinking and feeling but you can, with practice, manage these processes so that they help you perform to your best.

THOUGHT CONTROL

In the previous chapter a number of strategies were outlined for building and maintaining confidence. These included:

POSITIVE SELF-TALK
THOUGHT STOPPING
REFRAMING

These are, in effect, ways of taking control of your thoughts. Everybody has negative thoughts, but winners have learned to keep them to a minimum. They change their negative thoughts almost automatically without even realising they are doing it. They use these techniques all the time and just consider it common sense.

Greta Waitz, the great marathon runner, in an interview with a sport psychologist, was asked to describe her thoughts during races. She mentioned clearing her mind of negative thoughts when they occurred. The psychologist asked her if she practised thought stopping during training in preparation for races. She replied:

"Is that what you call it? I have always done this, even as a child."

You can also develop these techniques with practice. Practise these strategies as you train so that they become as ingrained as any physical skill. It may seem silly and over analytical at first, but give it time.

EXERCISE 4.4 Setting the scene

Write down some general thoughts that are likely to set the scene for a positive training session.

_____

_____

_____

e.g. *"I am in good form – I'm looking forward to trying something new – I'm training well."*

Write some of the negative thoughts that occur before or during training and reframe them.

_____

_____

_____

e.g. *"I hate stamina training"* ⟶ *"When the going gets tough, the tough get going."*

Write some goals for a training or practice session. Setting goals for training helps you exert more control. You can focus on things you have influence over.

_____

_____

_____

e.g. *"I will practise shooting by taking at least 20 shots at goal."*

These strategies for developing thought control become second nature when they are incorporated into regular training sessions and competitions. It is only through regular practice and application that they will be useful in pressure situations.

EMOTIONAL CONTROL

Most of the strategies for emotional control focus on calming the mind and reducing anxiety. There are some sports and occasions when psyching up is required, so some suggestions are outlined for those situations also.

The two most important points to make at the outset are: awareness of your mental and emotional state at all times is crucial to taking control; the strategies suggested need to be practised regularly if they are to be effective when most needed.

EXERCISE 4.5 **Calming techniques**

Breathing is a bridge between mind and body. Our breathing patterns are usually a reflection of our state of mind. When you are calm and relaxed your breathing is quiet and easy. When you are angry, tense, or upset you tend to hold your breath or take rapid short breaths. You can use breathing to calm the mind and body, especially when you feel like this. Exhalation, particularly long slow breaths, stimulates the part of the nervous system that calms the body.

Centred breathing

1. Place your hand on the centre of your abdomen. As you inhale let your abdomen expand. Your diaphragm relaxes as your stomach pushes out, thus allowing the lungs to fill up with more air than usual. Hold for two seconds.

2. Exhale slowly by pulling in your abdominal muscles, thus pushing the air out of your lungs. Pay more attention to this phase of the breathing.

3. As you exhale say the word "relax" quietly to yourself and let your shoulders and arms relax. Focus on expelling the muscular tension from the rest of the body with each subsequent breath.

4. After about five breaths you will feel the tension ease out of your body.

5. Centered breathing is the basis for most types of relaxation training.

It takes approximately four weeks of daily practice to get the real benefits from this technique. When you learn to use your abdominal muscles you do not need to place your hands on your stomach anymore. Audio tapes with guided instructions are useful when learning this technique (see Appendix 2). Use centered breathing on the way to or during training. Gradually incorporate it into critical periods in the training session, for example if you are getting frustrated. Progress to using it in competitive situations in the same way. Regular use of centered breathing will optimise its effectiveness.

Relaxation Exercises

Relaxation exercises are designed to relax and release the tension from the body and calm the mind. Relaxation is one of the key skills of mental training. Regular relaxation training contributes to overall mental fitness. The two types of relaxation exercises most commonly used are progressive muscular relaxation (PMR) and autogenics. PMR involves alternatively tightening and relaxing the main muscles to induce physical relaxation. This method is refered to as a muscle to mind technique, as the main focus is on relaxing the body first. Autogenics uses the mind to calm the body by consciously creating relaxed feelings throughout the body. This is known as a mind to muscle technique. Relaxation training is experiential and a number of tapes are available to help you develop this skill (see Appendix 2). The ability to relax is also the foundation for imagery exercises.

Coolness under pressure

During competition there will be occasions when you need to calm down or when you might need to take control quickly. These include crucial periods in the event, when trying too hard, when falling behind or after a major error. Here are some strategies that can help:

1. Slow down the play.
    If your sport allows you to slow the play down (e.g. a line ball, a service, a break in play, a time out), take this time to breathe slowly and reframe your internal dialogue.

2. Smile.
    If you are getting frustrated or angry, smiling often takes the heat out of the

situation. It can be a signal to ease off and enjoy the game more. After all, enjoyment is one of the emotions associated with performing well.

3. Cue words.

    Using cue words is a very effective technique during competition. Use words such as: 'cool it', 'slow down', 'stay calm'.

4. Stay in the present.

    Many people get uptight when they make mistakes, or think time is running out, or get mad at an umpire's decision. In a sense they are out of control. If this happens to you, click your fingers, use a cue word or slap your thigh as a signal to get back into the present.

5. Loosen up.

    If you feel your muscles are overtight then tense them a little more and just shake them out in a relaxed way. Repeat this several times until the tension eases. This overtightening of the muscles followed by a quick release reduces tension.

6. Choose your words.

    If you tend to get tense or anxious be careful of the wording in your thoughts or statements. Couching them in negative terms such as 'I hope I don't freeze', 'I will be okay, if I don't make a mistake early on' means you are focusing on what you don't want to happen. It is better to think about what you do want to happen.

EXERCISE 4.6 **Training under pressure**

The most effective way to cope with pressure is to train for it. Set up situations in training that simulate competition. Practise coming from behind, train at race pace, train with aggressive opponents, set up a game in which poor umpiring decisions are made. The list is endless.

Make a list of some simulation practices you can set up to prepare for competitive pressure. During these pressure situations use the mental training techniques that you have been practising. It is through these integrated types of practices that you prepare physically and mentally for competitive situations.

EXERCISE 4.7 **Overcoming flatness**

A person or team can be underactivated when they are:

> low in confidence or believe they are going to lose.
> overconfident or underestimate the opposition.
> poorly motivated or unenthusiastic.

Flatness or under-arousal can also contribute to poor or indifferent performances. Identify an occasion when you were under-aroused before a competition. Identify the reason why. When you detect this type of mood it is important to take control or the inevitable poor performance will follow. Here are some strategies to get activated:

1.   Warm up
     A thorough warm up is essential when you feel flat. Warming up the body can activate the mind.

2.   Cues
     Using words or actions that 'jizz' you up are effective and help you get focused. Words like *'fast'*, *'strong'*, *'tough'*, *'the best'* are useful. Actions like shadow boxing, physical contact or hitting a ball hard, also set the mood.

3.   Create a challenge
     Try out some new technique or tactic if the opposition is much weaker. It will give you something to focus on.

4.   Pep talk
     In team games a pep talk used judiciously can create a spirit and determination. Over-use of the pep talk can diminish its impact, so it is important to use it appropriately.

5.   Breathing.
     As mentioned earlier, breathing is a bridge to the mind. Just as exhalation can send signals to the nervous system to slow the body down, inhalation does the opposite. Have you noticed how people in power sports often use breathing to get activated. Short, sharp breaths send signals to the body to ready itself for action.

IMAGERY CONTROL

Imagery is the ability to recreate experiences using information stored in the memory and also to imagine future events. It is something everybody does naturally. Dreaming about scoring the winning goal in a cup final is imagery. Attempting to control this process for the purpose of improving performance is the essence of imagery control. It is often referred to as visualisation, mental rehearsal, or mental practice. These words give the impression that imagery depends only on the visual sense, but all the senses are involved when imagining is done well. The senses and feelings can be experienced during imagery exercises. It is possible, for example, to remember feelings of confidence and joy. During imagery, the senses can be used to recreate scenes, for example the feel of a ball and the sound of the crowd. Imagery is used in many of the exercises throughout this book. It is one of the essential mental training strategies.

Successful sportspeople use imagery to enhance their performance. It is a skill they have developed subconsciously. More and more people now realise its potential to aid sporting performance and they are deliberately developing imagery skills. Imagery can be used to enhance performance in a number of ways:

    to mentally rehearse specific skills.
    to recall previous positive performances to boost confidence.
    to correct areas of performance that are causing problems.
    to prepare for imminent events.
    to recover from injury.
    to imagine goals being achieved.

Tennis star Chris Evert in describing how she used imagery shows how powerful it can be:

"Before I play a match, I try to carefully rehearse what is likely to happen and how I will react in certain situations. I visualise myself playing typical points based on my opponent's style of play. I see myself hitting crisp deep shots from the baseline and coming to the net if I get a weak return. This helps me mentally prepare for a match and I feel like I've already played the match before I walk on court."

Going to the movies

Imagery is experienced in one or two ways. Internal imagery is seeing a situation from your own point of view. It is as if you are in the situation yourself. You can feel the movements as if they are actually happening. External imagery is seeing yourself from the perspective of an onlooker. It is like seeing yourself performing on screen. The important thing when doing an imagery exercise is to include as many senses as possible:

> *a clear image, with as much detail as possible, e.g. the arena*
> *hear the sounds, e.g. the contact of the ball on a racquet*
> *smell the scents, e.g. freshly cut grass*
> *feel the sensations, e.g. the feel of the track*
> *experience the emotion, e.g. the excitement of pre-match*

EXERCISE 4.9 **Imagining success**

Imagery exercises are very useful in overcoming a negative mindset. People often find it easier to imagine success, so combining this ability with regular physical practice is much more powerful than practising on a physical level only. Porter and Foster's book *Visual Athletics* (see Appendix 1) contains some good examples of scripts that can be used by coaches to guide imagery exercises. If you are self-coached you can record these scripts to make your own guided imagery tapes.

Ninety per cent of my game is mental.

IMPLICATIONS FOR COACHES

UNDERSTANDING

The first step in helping the people you coach exercise control is to develop an understanding of the crucial impact the mind has on performance. How individuals are feeling and what they are thinking and imagining creates an energy within that can lead to either a performance that is consistent with their ability or one that is extremely poor. The feelings that are likely to lead to performing well are challenge, security, excitement, pride, and when appropriate, fun. Do you as a coach help create these feelings with your people?

The feelings that are associated with inconsistent performances are fear, over-arousal (anxiety), under-arousal (flatness), frustration, boredom, and anger. Coaches need to identify when their performers feel like this and help them deal with these feelings.

Coaches should also be aware of the relationship of thoughts to performance. Negative, pessimistic, and unrealistic thoughts usually have an adverse affect on performance in training and competition.

Do you look out for signs of negative thinking? Are you aware of the thoughts that your athletes or players have, particularly about competition? It is only when you develop an awareness and understanding of the impact of thoughts and feelings that you can help people deal with them in appropriate ways.

MODELLING

The most effective way to teach control is to model it yourself. Performers are more likely to take on board what you say if you also practise what you preach. As the Americans say, "Walk your talk." If you lose control by getting angry or anxious, or express your negative thoughts regularly, then expect the people you coach to catch some of them. Even though you may not express your feelings or thoughts verbally, your body language will give them away. Coaches should consider if their words or behaviour have any negative impact on their athletes' or players' performance. If so they should make appropriate changes.

Opposite: Chris Evert

Are you aware of your own thoughts and feelings when you are coaching?

What are your thoughts and feelings on the day of competition?

Do you practise what you preach consistently?

In an interview before one of the play-off matches for the 1998 World Cup, Irish soccer manager Mick McCarthy illustrated this well.

"I think it's important that I appear relaxed as well. Sometimes, before a big game, it's easy for the coach or manager to have a panic attack. You can bring them in and start fussing: 'We better do this or we better do that or we'll do it differently this time'."

I think it's important that I appear relaxed as well

OBSERVING AND LISTENING

If you are a coach who understands the role of mental fitness in sport and you wish to help people improve their control in this area then a good starting point is developing your own observation and listening skills. Too often coaches are talking so much that they do not hear or see what is really going on. Be vigilant for the signs of poorly developed mental fitness (see page 28). A coach, for example can notice a performer who gets over-anxious before events by looking out for:

Change in usual behaviour, e.g. becoming very quiet or very noisy.
Paleness of the skin, particularly the face.
More frequent visits to the toilet than usual.
Complaints about not feeling right.

CREATE A POSITIVE ENVIRONMENT

People thrive in a supportive, encouraging and positive environment. Too often coaching is over-concerned with highlighting faults or punishing inappropriate behaviour. Rewarding effort and positive behaviour creates an atmosphere where people are not afraid to make mistakes. Positive coaching is more likely to produce people who are confident and in control.

SUMMARY

Of all the factors that influence how you perform in your sport, your own internal environment is the one over which you can exert most control. Your thoughts, feelings and images are at the centre of your internal environment and these mental processes have a direct effect on a multitude of physical functions and behaviour. The essence of control is taking charge of these mental processes to create an internal environment that is conducive to performing well consistently. Strategies for thought control include, positive self-talk, thought stopping and re-framing. Calming techniques are crucial for maintaining or regaining emotional control. Feelings of fear, anxiety or anger have the potential to hinder sports performers; therefore developing techniques to regulate them is of tremendous benefit. Another powerful strategy in developing control is imagery. Using images, memories of feelings, and the senses, it is possible to create positive experiences in the mind. This can be used to complement skill and tactical work, solve problems, prepare for forthcoming events, and as an aid to injury recovery.

Opposite: Mick McCarthy

My greatest opponent is my mind:
my poor attention span and impatience

Chapter 5

IMPROVING CONCENTRATION

WHAT IS CONCENTRATION?

RATE YOUR ABILITY TO CONCENTRATE

STRATEGIES TO IMPROVE CONCENTRATION

IMPLICATIONS FOR COACHES

Opposite: Ken Doherty, World Champion 1997

Had we kept cool and concentrated on keeping possession we would have survived

"We were four points up and we started to panic a little.
Had we kept cool and concentrated on keeping possession
we would have survived."
(Ger Power, after the 1982 All Ireland Football Final,
which Kerry lost to Offaly.)

"Ninety per cent of my game is mental.
It's my concentration that has gotten me this far."
(Chris Evert, tennis player at the height of her career.)

How many times do you hear people telling others to concentrate or complaining about loss of concentration. Concentration is so much part of sport it is taken for granted. So much so that defining it precisely is rarely done.

Concentration is a mental ability like the other components of mental fitness. It is the ability to direct attention to relevant cues or information and maintain attention for the appropriate amount of time.

The two key aspects to concentration are direction of attention and maintenance of attention.

DIRECTION OF ATTENTION

A sportsperson has to contend with vast amounts of information and cues every time he or she trains or competes. Such things as opponents, the weather, the venue, the score, the time, personal thoughts, the crowd, the coach, the pattern of the game, the referee, and thoughts of winning or losing are vying for attention throughout the training session or event. Think of other cues that apply to your sport.

Opposite: Ger Power

The nature of most sports means that your attention has to shift constantly as the cues change. Developing the ability to focus on the relevant cues is learned and like any skill it needs practice. There are four main ways in which you can direct your attention:

1. A broad focus means attending to several cues at one time. In sports such as team games, slalom canoeing, and mountain biking the environment is changing rapidly, and responding to the relevant cues is crucial.

2. A narrow focus means attending to only one or two relevant cues. Taking a penalty, receiving a serve, or waiting for the gun to go are examples.

3. An external focus means attending to cues in the environment such as the ball, an opponent, or the wind.

4. An internal focus means attending to personal cues such as your thoughts or feelings – thinking about which way you are going to kick a penalty or what type of serve you are going to deliver.

You can see that concentration is not one-dimensional. It is constantly changing in response to the cues in the environment. So your attention can be directed in a number of ways.

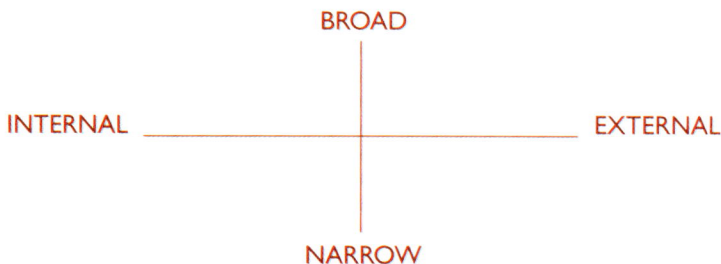

BROAD

INTERNAL _____|_____ EXTERNAL

NARROW

Here are two examples to illustrate how shifting the direction of your attention occurs in an event

The first one could apply to most team games.

Just before the start of the game, the team captain talks to the coach about which way they will play if they win the toss. His attention is broad-external, focusing on the weather, previous experience, the advice of the coach, and the time. When the toss is over he moves to mark his opponent, his attention is still broad but shifts internally for a few moments as he gets himself ready for action. After a few minutes his opponent scores. His attention is now narrow (*"What foot did he kick with? How did he get past me?"*) and internal (*"I will give him less space next time and I will keep him on his left side."*).

As the game restarts after the score his attention is still internal as he reminds himself to get on with it and not dwell on the score, but it is also broader again as he assesses his position and where the ball might land.

The second example illustrates how crucial directing attention appropriately is. Often referred to as focus.

At the 1995 European Swimming Championships Michelle Smith won a silver medal in her first race – the 400 individual medley. Everybody was talking about the possibility of gold in the next race – the 100m butterfly, after she was fastest qualifier for the final. She finished fifth and had this to say afterwards:

> *"Going into the final I realised for the first time I had the chance of winning a gold medal at international level. That unsettled me. I forgot about my own race. It was a painful lesson."*

A couple of days later in the 200 she won the gold and showed how valuable that lesson was:

> *"I concentrated in the final on swimming my own race, not bothering with anyone else or thinking of what they were doing. I did not look around me at any stage, even though in the last 50 metres it was tempting to sneak a look. I kept my head down and kept going without knowing my placing until I had touched the wall."*

MAINTENANCE OF ATTENTION

Maintaining concentration for the duration of the training session or event is equally important. Sports vary enormously in duration, thus placing different demands on the performer's concentration. It is important to examine the nature of your sport in terms of its concentration demands. The examples below will help you.

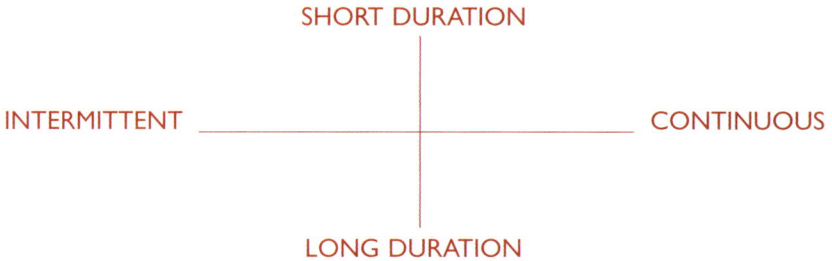

SHORT DURATION

INTERMITTENT _____|_____ CONTINUOUS

LONG DURATION

Examples of sports in each category:

Short-continuous: Sprint events, dressage, gymnastics

Short-intermittent: Judo, shooting, weight-lifting

Long-continuous: Cycling, long distance running

Long-intermittent: Football, court games, golf

EXERCISE 5.1   **Concentration demands**

Think about the nature and duration of your sport. What are the concentration demands associated with this activity?

_____

_____

IMPORTANCE OF CONCENTRATION

At the highest levels of sport there is little difference in fitness levels, skill, tactical awareness, commitment, confidence and self-control between the competitors. The difference between them on a given day is often due to concentration. Take professional golf as an example. Over ten tournaments the difference between the top money earner and a player further down the list may be only 20 shots. This is after 30 to 35 rounds of golf with each player taking approximately 2,500 shots.

In team games, where 20 to 40 games may be played in a league during the season, the difference between the teams fighting out promotion may be only a couple of points. Looking back over the season there will probably be a few matches that were lost or drawn because of lapses in concentration.

The ability to concentrate is vital in all sports. In sports of short duration a lapse in concentration can mean there is no time to recover. After months of training, particularly in the physical and technical aspects, the whole season can end because of lack of mental preparation, especially on the skill of concentration.

In sports where concentration has to be maintained over long periods the danger of distractions is even greater. The ability to stay focused can be the crucial element in the quality of athlete or team performances. The intermittent sports also provide a challenge to the sportsperson's powers of concentration. The ability to focus attention during the crucial times and then relax between play is just as important as any physical skill.

Cricketer Ian Botham described this ability:

"I channel my concentration into just a few seconds before each ball is bowled. Then I switch off, and perhaps have a laugh or joke with the other slips and the wicket-keeper, or even the batsman. It helps me and my mates because it keeps them relaxed, and so they don't get tired or bored easily if we're having a hard time of it."

LEARNING TO CONCENTRATE

As with the other mental qualities of commitment, confidence and control the ability to concentrate is learned. People in sport assume that if you yell at somebody to concentrate then they will automatically obey. If only it were that simple! The most effective way to develop concentration is through sustained practice of the strategies presented later in this chapter.

The first thing to bear in mind is that concentration is related very closely to your general mental fitness. Although concentration is being dealt with here as a separate quality it is influenced very strongly by each of the other aspects of mental fitness. Think about competitions you took part in where your commitment was low. You probably were unfocused also. When motivation is higher and an event is more important, you tend to concentrate harder. The same is true with confidence. Low confidence usually leads to difficulty concentrating. It is also easy to understand how loss of control such as anxiety, anger, or negative thinking affects concentration. Therefore, the better developed your overall mental fitness is, the more focused your concentration will be.

Inappropriate focus is the main problem for sportspeople where concentration is concerned. Essentially the mind is not focusing on the relevant cues at a given time in the competition. Sportspeople get distracted by other cues in the environment or their own thoughts and emotions. We see many examples of this.

One person who can verify this is snooker player Ken Doherty. For years he was recognised as a world-class player who had not delivered on the big occasions. A few months before he became World Champion in 1997 he suffered a humiliating defeat to Steve Davis. In an interview afterwards he mentioned one problem that he needed to work on if he was to make a breakthrough:

"My greatest opponent is my mind: my poor attention span and impatience. It may look like the strongest part of my game when you watch me on the telly because I'm quite intense looking when I'm out there. But my mind wanders and sometimes it falls asleep and I'll play a silly shot at the wrong time, be a bit lackadaisical with an easy pot or play a safety shot too quickly."

RATE YOUR ABILITY TO CONCENTRATE

Concentration is influenced by both external and internal factors.

EXERCISE 5.2 **Identify external factors**

Make a list of the main cues in the environment that you need to focus on as well as those that could distract you during a competition.

_____

_____

If you have been thorough you will notice that there are many powerful distractions fighting for your attention. Things that may be inappropriate to focus on include the venue, the weather, spectators, opponents, officials, and umpires. In some sports it will be important to assess the effects of some of these cues on how you will play, but it is important not to be distracted by them.

It is also important to do this exercise for training. The habits developed at training are usually carried into competition.

Brent Pope, a New Zealander coaching Clontarf rugby team, had this to say about Irish players when he came to work in Dublin:

> *"Here people expect to come down on a Thursday night, throw a couple of balls, jump a couple of times and then complain on a Saturday when the throws aren't straight or the passes are bad or the kicks have missed touch."*

You cannot eliminate the environmental cues but you can become aware of their power to distract you. With so many potential distractions you can see why it is important to develop strategies to focus on the relevant cues. The next exercise deals with another major source of potential distractions: your internal environment. Your thoughts and feelings are the main elements of your internal environment.

Identify internal factors

Make a list of the internal factors, i.e. thoughts, emotions or images that affect your concentration during competitions. Do a separate list for training sessions.

_____

_____

Thoughts have immense power to distract. As mentioned in earlier chapters, you cannot entirely eliminate thoughts, but you need to take control of them if they are not to sabotage your performance. There are three types of thoughts that have the potential to distract your attention and therefore we can call them irrelevant cues.

THOUGHTS ABOUT THE PAST

Focusing on memories of previous competitions can be distracting as you approach a current event. You may not have performed very well at that venue or against a particular opponent. On the other hand you may have always beaten a particular opponent or team and you may not be fully tuned in for today.

One of the most common distractions during competition is thinking about an error you have made. You may have fumbled a ball that led to a score, you may have hit a poor shot, missed an easy score, or made a tactical error; you keep blaming yourself or thinking about the mistake for a long time afterwards. While you are distracted by those thoughts other crucial cues are being missed as the competition proceeds.

It is not only errors that cause your mind to wander. Sometimes you can be distracted by thoughts of what you have done well. Very often in sport we see a great score cancelled out almost immediately because players have not focused as the opposition re-start or counter-attack.

THOUGHTS ABOUT THE FUTURE

Equally distracting as thoughts about the past are thoughts about the future. Instead of staying in the present many sportspeople get distracted when they are in the lead. They begin to think about how long is left and what can they do to protect their lead. Everybody can think of an example where a person in the lead started thinking too much about the consequences of what they were doing and so lost rhythm and momentum. Competitors who fall behind in the closing stages can also make errors of judgement due to thoughts about the outcome.

THOUGHTS ABOUT TECHNIQUE

It is common in technical sports for people to start analysing their technique during competitions. This over-analysis of mechanics distracts participants to such an extent that they miss the more relevant cues. Jack Nicklaus used to ask golfers:

"What's your picture of golf? Do you see it as an exercise in club swinging and ball striking, or as a game decided by numbers on a scoreboard?"

He believed many amateur golfers suffered from paralysis by analysis, meaning they were over-analysing their swing instead of focusing on the shot.

Other elements of the internal environment that affect concentration are emotions, physical fitness, and well-being. We have shown already how emotions such as fear, anxiety, and anger can impact on performance. These emotions also affect concentration. Low levels of physical fitness also have an adverse effect on concentration. As a sportsperson gets tired or is suffering due to inadequate levels of fitness for the demands of the competition, his or her concentration tends to become distracted. Preoccupation with an injury or illness is also potentially distracting.

Developing the ability to focus on relevant cues and block out distractions for the duration of training or competition is essential to becoming a consistent performer. It is an ability that is learned over time. The strategies to develop concentration are designed to be incorporated into your existing training schedules.

I channel my concentration into just a few seconds before each ball is bowled

STRATEGIES TO IMPROVE CONCENTRATION

Many of the strategies described previously are also useful to develop concentration. Using these strategies consistently over time means you get into habits that improve your mental fitness. Without realising it these strategies become automatic and you use them during training and competition. They become part of your routine.

EXERCISE 5.4 **Set goals**

Setting performance goals helps to focus your attention at training and in competitions (see pages 47 and 48).

Set appropriate goals for your next training session.

_____

_____

Set appropriate goals for your next competition.

_____

_____

EXERCISE 5.5 **Pre-competition routine**

Most sportspeople have routines, especially on days of competition. These include specific meals, wearing certain clothes, travelling arrangements, routines in the changing room, and finally a warm-up. These routines can help to focus attention if used consistently. Developing a pre-competition routine and a competition plan are two strategies that lay the foundation for a focused mind.

Opposite: Ian Botham

List out the activities that you need to carry out on the days leading up to a competition. Continue the list to include the night before and the actual day. These include travel arrangements, registration, meals, packing your bag, team talks, and other details that are relevant to your sport. This will help you arrive at the competition site relaxed, ready, and focused.

_____

_____

_____

In the weeks leading up to the 1995 All Ireland Football Final, Dublin manager Pat O'Neill used this idea as part of overall preparation:

"We moved the Saturday training sessions to the precise time of the game and ran things according to the match timetable. It gave their bodies and minds a dress rehearsal for the big day and established a tempo."

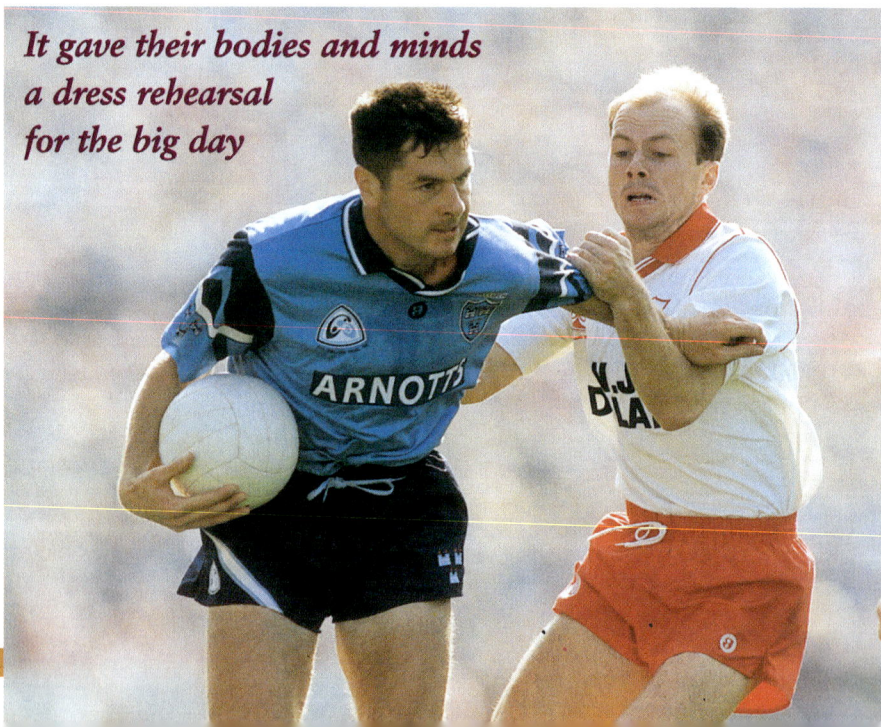

It gave their bodies and minds a dress rehearsal for the big day

The warm-up is the final phase of you pre-competition routine. A thorough warm-up not only gets your body ready for the tasks ahead, it also helps to focus your mind. Think about your preparation in the hour before you compete and then outline the content and sequence of your routine. The key question to ask yourself at this stage is 'how do I feel?' If you feel flat you need to use the activation strategies (page 102) or if you are over-anxious you need to focus on calming techniques (page 99).

_____

_____

Here is an example relevant to most team sports:

Physical / Technical	**Mental / Tactical**
CHANGING ROOM	
Dress and check equipment	Relax and chat with team-mates
Limber up and stretch	Positive self-talk
Skill rehearsal	Reminder of your goal
IN THE ARENA	
More vigorous warm-up	Start to narrow your focus
Skill work, e.g. shooting	Relaxed breathing

EXERCISE 5.6 **Competition plan**

You cannot plan for everything that is going to happen in a competition but you can prepare for most things. It is often said *"by failing to prepare, you are preparing to fail"*. In **Exercise 5.4.** you set performance goals for competition day. Now build on these by outlining a plan of how you would like to perform. For example, take an early lead, adapt a certain tactic, come strong in the second half.

_____

_____

Opposite: Action from the 1995 All-Ireland Football Final

REFOCUSING

It is almost inevitable that your concentration will slip during an event. That is the nature of sport and that is what makes competition so absorbing. Usually concentration is lost at certain periods or after critical situations.

Critical situation	Preferred response
Going a goal behind	Restart quickly and stick to original game-plan
Coming close to halfway in a race	Increase the pace for 400m
False start	Walk back slowly and focus on start
Make a critical mistake	Let it go and focus on the play
Disagreement with official	Smile and apologise
Inclement weather	Positive self-talk and reframe negative thoughts
In the lead with 5 mins left	Stay focused on the present and do my job well

EXERCISE 5.7 Identify critical situations

List some of the critical situations and periods you are likely to face within your competition. Then decide how you would like to respond to them.

_____

_____

The ability to refocus your attention to revelant cues is a vital part of concentration. You can visualise yourself making the appropriate response in the days leading up to a competition. You are planting seeds in your mind, which give you a better chance of repeating what you have planned on the day.

The ability to stay focused is developed with practice. Tennis player Bjorn Borg was one of the best examples of a focused athlete throughout his career. He developed his extraordinary powers of concentration with help from his parents. In later years when he was asked about the reason for his success he replied:

"It was my ability to play one point at a time and not worry and think about what just happened or what might happen. The only thing that was important was the point about to be played."

This ability to stay in the present can be developed by anybody. It means focusing on the present shot or the current segment of play. The importance of blocking out or letting go of the past was mentioned earlier. Errors can have a powerful effect on concentration, therefore developing the ability to stay in the present is one solution to this problem. Equally destructive is thinking ahead sometimes. Too often in sport we witness individuals or teams getting caught in the dying seconds of an event. It is likely that their attention has drifted to the finish line, the final whistle, the winning point or the last move a little bit too early.

Two additional techniques that help maintain concentration and aid refocusing are trigger words and reminders.

EXERCISE 5.8   **Trigger words**

Motivational: *'push it' – 'go for it' – 'attack'*

Instructional: *'eyes on the ball' – 'swing easy' – 'follow through'*

Think of motivational or instructional trigger words that you can use. The motivational words are used when you are trying to get extra effort from yourself. The instructional words can be useful if you need to refocus after a mistake or to shift to an internal focus before a shot.

Motivational Words_____

Instructional Words _____

Then consider specific times when you could use them in competitions.

To put them into practice, introduce them in training followed by less important competitions. Finally implement them in all competitions.

Reminders

We have already said that the essence of concentration is paying attention to the relevant cues at the right time. Identify cues that are important to focus on in your sport. Examples of relevant cues include the ball, your opponent, the course or the target.

_____

_____

When you feel your attention slipping develop a technique that is suitable to refocus. This might be slapping your thigh, clicking your fingers, or kicking the ground. You need to practise this in training if it is to be of benefit in competition. Identify a technique to help you refocus.

_____

_____

DEVELOPING CONCENTRATION

You have identified the concentration demands of your sport in **Exercise 5.1**. To prepare adequately for competition you need to simulate the demands of the competitions during part of or all your training sessions. This helps develop your ability to direct attention to the relevant cues and maintain your concentration for an appropriate length of time.

EXERCISE 5.10 **Simulation training**

Think about the way you train and list out drills or practices that you can include in your training sessions that simulate the demands of competition.

_____

_____

_____

Here are some examples highlighting the mental ability that can be developed

Simulated practice	Mental ability being developed
Sparring for combat sports	Sustain concentration for the length of a competitive bout. Cope with a variety of opponents.
Go through your full pre-event routine the week before an important competition	To narrow focus in the period before the competition begins.

EXERCISE 5.11   **Distraction training**

When you are used to training at competitive pace you need to add in the element of surprise that can occur in a competition. From previous exercises you know what potential distractions can affect you during competition. Set up practices where these distractions occur. During these practices use whatever technique is most suitable for you to regain your focus. If you train on your own you may need to bring somebody along to introduce the element of surprise.

Distraction
Losing your cool at a poor umpiring decision.

Practice
Set up a game in training where the umpire deliberately makes some bad calls without the players' knowledge.

Technique to refocus
Use breathing out or a trigger word like 'stay calm' as a cue to relax.

Distraction
In equestrian events your horse gets upset if there is a crowd or noise.

Practice
Go through your warm-up in an indoor arena with music playing and people moving about.

Technique to refocus
Stay in the present until the horse settles. Then start slowly at first allowing the horse to get accustomed to the noise and the movement.

Coaches have a responsibility to help develop their performers' ability to concentrate as much as any other aspect of performance. Coaches can assist their athletes in the identification of key cues to focus on and techniques to refocus when they get distracted. This work is done in training during simulation and distraction practices and not just by talking about it. Therefore, planning training sessions and involving the athletes is essential in order to get maximum benefit.

DRILLS AND SKILLS

Coaches often use drills to rehearse and practise skills. Sometimes the drills are designed to develop an aspect of physical fitness also. With some thought and planning you can incorporate mental training into your drills. Think of ways in which you can improve concentration during drills. Encourage the participants to use trigger words, reminders, and self-talk to maintain their concentration or to refocus when they lose it.

TRAINING GOALS

Set goals for each training session and remind participants about the goal throughout the session. Encourage and assist them all to set their own goals and check with them regularly to ensure they are keeping up this practice.

ROUTINES

As a coach you should assist your athletes to develop pre-competition plans. Help them with these and practise the routine or part of it in training so that it is second nature to them on the day of competition.

FEEDBACK

The nature of training and competition is such that concentration will vary greatly during each. Coaches should look for signs of concentration lapses as much as any other aspects of the sport. Note what you see and the consequence of the lapse and then discuss it with the individual afterwards, help the athlete to identify a technique to address the lapse.

Opposite: Denis Hickie, Irish rugby player

Teach or reinforce the technique that can help the performer with his or her concentration. In the next event or training session include the technique, look out for signs of improvement and give feedback to the performer. Observation, correction, and feedback are the essence of coaching. This is the means by which the technical and tactical aspects of sports are coached and it is also the way to teach the mental strategies described in this book.

The habits of training carry over to the match

SUMMARY

Concentration is the ability to direct your attention to relevant cues or information and maintain your attention for the appropriate amount of time. Concentration constantly shifts in response to internal and external cues and the changing environment. Sports also vary enormously in duration, thus placing different demands on athletes' concentration. The ability to concentrate is learned. Using strategies like trigger words and reminders at training and then in competition is part of this learning process. Simulation and distraction practices also help develop concentration. Pre-competition routines focus attention in the lead-up to an event and when these are combined with a competition plan and re-focusing techniques you have a range of strategies that lead to improved concentration.

I am only one cog
in a big wheel, but
an important one.
I think it is good
to think like that

Chapter 6

THE ROAD TO MENTAL FITNESS

THE IMPORTANCE OF MENTAL FITNESS

BARRIERS TO MENTAL TRAINING

IMPLEMENTING A MENTAL TRAINING PLAN

DESIGNING A MENTAL TRAINING PROGRAMME

Opposite: Yuri Djorkoeff, member of the French soccer team - World Champions 1998

Many athletes have extraordinary physical skills and attributes but the great ones have equally extraordinary psychological skills

THE IMPORTANCE OF MENTAL FITNESS

Although mental fitness is only one aspect of performing well in sport, it plays such a vital part that to neglect mental preparation is leaving you ill-equipped to perform to the best of your ability. Most people involved in sport can think of occasions when they under-performed due to mental factors. This can be frustrating when you have spent so much time training and preparing. All too often the preparation has focused only on physical fitness and skills practice. Frequently it is a lack of mental preparation that contributes to less than satisfactory performances. Can you identify with any of these experiences? These are all situations that can be overcome with regular mental training:

failed to perform in the most important match of the season?

choked at a critical point in a competition?

lost concentration at training or when competing?

put yourself down before, during or after a competition?

found it difficult to get motivated?

lacked confidence in your ability?

found yourself tightening up due to nerves?

unable to get rid of negative thoughts?

been overcome with anger, fear or anxiety before or during a competition?

suffered from burn-out?

perform better at training than in competition?

Opposite: DJ Carey, Kilkenny hurler and multiple All-Ireland medalist

In every level of sport, competitors are often evenly matched in terms of physical fitness, skill and tactics. On competition day the difference between them is usually mental fitness. To illustrate this, compare the different mental approaches of Angela Chalmers and Sonia O'Sullivan, third and fourth respectively in the 1992, 3000m Olympic Final. Chalmers, an experienced competitor just edged out O'Sullivan who was competing for the first time at this level, by a fraction of a second.

Here is Chalmers account of her mental approach before and during the race.

(Before) *"The day before the race, Wynn (her coach) and I pulled out the race prep notebook (prepared prior to the Games). We looked at the women in the race and planned accordingly. I was very relaxed and confident when I lined up for my race. In the final minutes before the gun went off I repeated a few of the key words I wanted to use in the race."*

(During) *"I regained my composure by repeating my key words and reminding myself that I was tough, strong and relaxed."*

Here are O Sullivan's reflections of that day.

(Before) *"All day long I was subconsciously nervous, I couldn't concentrate on any one thing for more than five minutes. I tried to read, I tried to write postcards but nothing could hold my attention. Finally it was time to go to the track. I sat in the warm-up area for a half hour, drank water and ran to the port-a-loo about five times."*

(During) *"The race was moving so slowly, we were packed tightly together and it seemed to be taking forever. This was definitely a waiting game, but before I knew it there were only 300m to go. I was in the lead even though I didn't want to be leading until the final straight. With 100m to go I grew scared, I was looking for shadows. Suddenly I was swallowed up, I saw gold, then silver, then I was grabbing for bronze. Everything tightened up and I finished 4th. I never dreamt I would be 4th. I didn't have a bad race, but I didn't reach in far enough to take everything. It all just passed me by so quickly, I don't remember how it unfolded like it did."*
(From Sonia's diary: Irish Runner Annual 1993.)

Sonia O'Sullivan clearly learned from this experience as she went on to become World 5,000m champion in 1995 and double World Cross Country champion in 1998. This ability to learn from experience and recover positively from setbacks is also a hallmark of successful competitors.

BARRIERS TO MENTAL TRAINING

Throughout the book it has been emphasised that mental fitness is learned and you can benefit from using the strategies described in each chapter no matter what age you are, what sport you play and at whatever level you compete. All you need is a willingness, an open mind and a persistence to follow through, to enjoy the benefits of mental training. Unfortunately many sportspeople and coaches still neglect mental preparation. If you are one of these people it is worth reflecting on the reasons for this. There are six common reasons put forth for neglecting mental training. They are:

LACK OF KNOWLEDGE

It is common to hear people shout commands like '*concentrate*', '*relax*', '*cool it*' or '*push it*', to competitors. The assumption being that they know how to do it and they just need a reminder. This has been the extent of mental training for many sportspeople because it was not understood that mental fitness could be improved through regular training. Now that mental fitness is an integral part of coach education programmes and books are widely available on the subject, lack of knowledge should not be as big a barrier as it may have been in the past.

Some people think that mental fitness is best taught by specialists such as sports psychologists, and they may not feel competent in their own knowledge or ability in this area. You do not have to be a psychologist to use psychology. Coaches and sportspeople have employed many of the mental training techniques over the years and you can follow in their footsteps. The way to become competent is through practice and like any new skill it takes time to become proficient.

MENTAL FITNESS IS INNATE

It is assumed by many that successful sportspeople are born rather than made; they were blessed with a psychological disposition that geared them for success. Although we are all born with a unique blend of physical and psychological qualities, it is the experiences we encounter through our lives that shapes our temperament. The central message from this book is that mental fitness is learned and it can be enhanced through effective and regular practice.

IT IS ONLY FOR ELITE PERFORMERS

The majority of people who take part in sport like to do their best. They practise to become more skillful and proficient. They train to become physically fitter. Nobody tells them not to do this because it is only for elite people. Mental training likewise can be incorporated into anybody's training.

IT IS ONLY FOR PROBLEM ATHLETES

The words mental and psychology conjure up images of someone who is messed up or has problems for many people. So it is natural that some people are suspicious or believe that sports psychology deals with problem athletes. Psychological problems do exist in sport, such as eating disorders, substance abuse and chronic depression. People with these type of problems are dealt with by personnel with an appropriate clinical background. The development of mental fitness comes under the scope of educational sport psychology. The basis of the educational approach is that if we can highlight the mental qualities that make consistent peak performers special, then we can teach these to others in the belief that it will help them perform to the best of their ability more often. So a sport psychologist or anybody else using this approach is really *a stretch* as opposed to the misconceived notion of *a shrink*.

IT IS NOT NECESSARY

It was mentioned in the introduction that to some the mention of mental fitness suggests hocus-pocus; others dismiss as weak-minded the competitor who needs such mental training. Because mental training is a relatively new addition to sports preparation it can still be viewed with suspicion by some. The same was the case when new methods of physical training were introduced. When these were seen to contribute to success there was widespread acceptance and the same is happening with mental training.

LACK OF TIME

This is usually a weak argument for not incorporating mental training into the overall preparation. If you believe mental fitness is important to performing to your potential and this is something you desire you will find time. Similarly, if you coach and you know how to develop mental fitness you will want to make it a priority, even in the time you have available.

IMPLEMENTING A MENTAL TRAINING PROGRAMME

There are a number of questions to consider before you incorporate mental training into your overall programme.

What are you trying to achieve?

When is the best time to implement it?

How do you implement it?

What are you trying to achieve?

Establishing your reasons for embracing mental training is vital because it will determine the success of your programme. The two most prevalent reasons for people becoming interested in mental fitness are: to solve a problem or to enjoy the benefits that accrue from regular mental training. The typical problems that people hope can be solved include, loss of form, overcoming competitive nerves or in the lead up to a big event. The expectation may be that a talk or meeting may offer a quick solution. While a once-off talk may be beneficial, in cases like these there is no guarantee that it will make any difference. This is an unrealistic expectation and shows a misunderstanding of mental fitness. As a coach you would not expect a new technique or tactic to be effective if it was introduced without time to practise a week before a final. The same logic should be applied to mental training. So if a problem is to be solved a longer term approach needs to be adopted. The same applies for those interested in enhancing their performance and enjoying the benefits of mental training.

When is the best time to implement mental training?

Think for a moment when you would introduce or emphasise other aspects of training such as skills practice, physical fitness development or tactical planning. You will see from the examples on pages 140 and 141 that most coaches divide a season into phases. Each phase has a purpose and the sum of the phases forms the overall training plan for the year. The most suitable phase to introduce a mental training programme is pre-season or early in the season. There is less pressure to compete and more time for practice. The time needed to integrate mental training into the overall training regime will vary greatly but generally it will take a number of months of regular practice to benefit significantly from new approaches. If mental training is introduced mid-season or at any time in response to a crisis, allow time for it to bear fruit. You would not expect to be physically fit after two training sessions. The same holds true for mental training.

How to implement mental training

In implementing a mental training programme refer to the steps on page 31. Set up a meeting at the start of a season to draw up goals and establish how committed people are (see page 39). This is a good time to create awareness of mental fitness, showing how it affects performance and outlining how it can be enhanced through mental training. This should ideally be backed up by a video or interview with well known personalities who have testified to or described the benefits of mental fitness. Descriptions of poor performances that resulted from lack of mental preparation are also helpful. This is also an opportunity for the participants to ask questions, clear up misconceptions and understand that mental training is beneficial to their performance.

A further meeting may be held to assess the athlete or team to build up a profile (see page 40). This will establish strengths, areas for improvement and an insight into what needs to be included in the programme. You are now at the stage to put together a training programme for the season. See the examples on pages 140 and 141.

When you have fun you can do amazing things

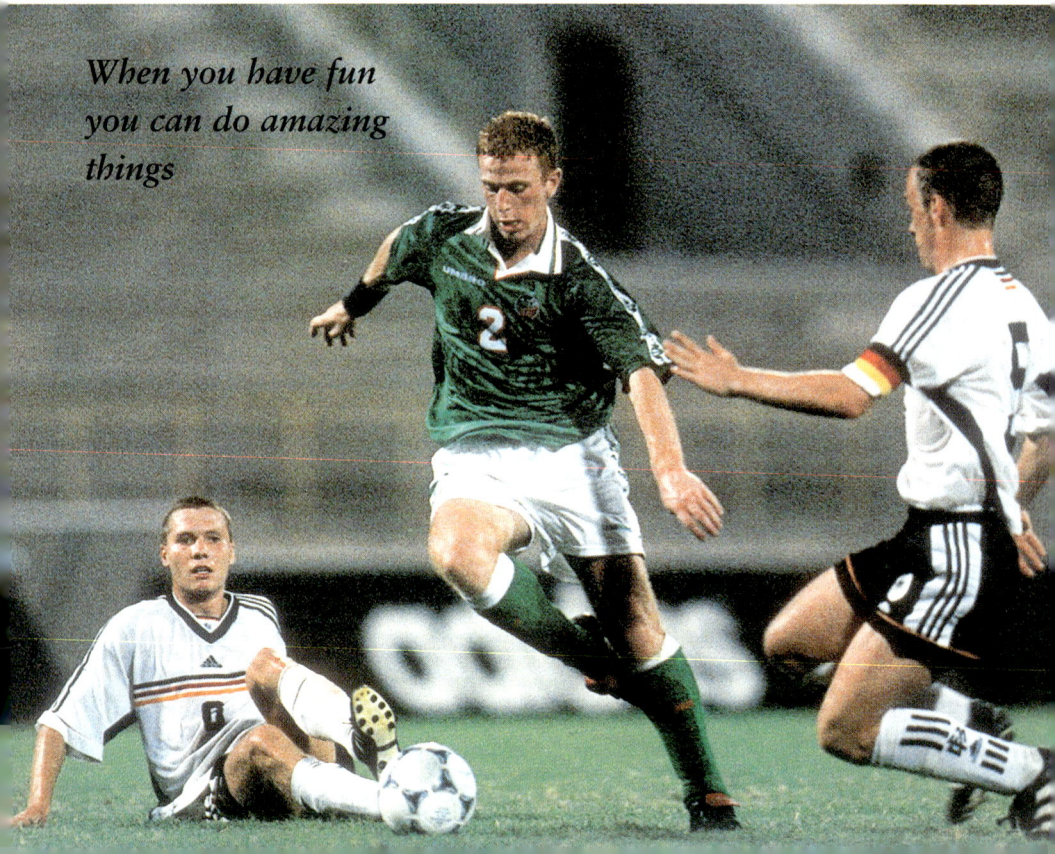

DESIGNING A MENTAL TRAINING PROGRAMME

Training plans are designed to help people achieve their goals. Knowledge, experience and understanding are combined to select what you think are the most suitable methods to achieve your goals. When goals have been set, a season plan is drawn up. The major competitions are written in and then the year is divided up to suit your programme. A thorough training programme includes work in the four main areas: physical fitness, mental fitness, technical development and tactical development.

The example below shows how a plan was drawn up for a 1500m runner. The overall goal was set first. Some short and long term goals were agreed. These were based on weaknesses identified in a pre-season assessment and their relevance to the major goal. The full programme is shown on page 140.

SEASON GOAL: To break 4.10 minutes by July.

PROFILE: Current best 4.16

GOALS: PHYSICAL FITNESS
               need to work on stamina.
               - increase mileage by 10% up to December.
               - introduce one interval session at race pace.
               TECHNICAL
               need to relax the shoulders more particularly at the end
               of races.
                - introduce drills to develop good running form.
               TACTICAL
               need to run at a more even pace, tendency to start too fast.
               - run in under and overdistance work-outs and races
               to develop pace judgement.
               MENTAL
               too anxious before races and a tendency to think negatively.
               - practise calming techniques and work on self-talk.

Opposite: Thomas Heary, member of Irish soccer team - U18 European Champions 1998

A SEASON TRAINING PROGRAMME FOR A 1500M RUNNER
OVERALL GOAL – TO RUN 4.10 IN JULY

Months	S O N D J F M A M J J A				
Phase	Conditioning	Specific conditioning	Pre competition	Competition	Transition
Competitions	1 or 2 cross country races	Regional & National C.C Championships	Opening track races in May	Regional & National Track Championships	No competitions
Physical fitness	Develop aerobic fitness	Increase long runs More race paced intervals	Introduce track sessions	Emphasis on race pace & speed	Active rest eg. swimming
Technical development	Working with weights for upper body	Relax shoulders in races	Drills to enhance technique	Continue drills	
Tactical development	Running even-paced intervals	Start at even pace in races	Running at different paces on track sessions	Run over and under distance to learn pace judgement	
Mental fitness	Goal-setting Centered breathing	Practise calming before races	Monitor self-talk Examine beliefs	Implement calming & positive self-talk at races	Re-evaluation Reading

A SEASON TRAINING PROGRAMME FOR A TEAM
OVERALL GOAL – TO GAIN PROMOTION (SEE PAGE 50)

Months	D J F	M A M J	J A S O	N
Phase	Conditioning	Pre-competition	Competition	Transition
Competitions	Early challenge games	Start of league games	Continuation of league Knockout competition	No competitions
Physical fitness	Assessment Steady runs and interval runs Flexibility	Re-assessment shorter intervals drills with the balls	Speed work	Active rest eg. cycling
Technical development	Basic skills practice at the start of a session	Emphasis on tackling	All round skill practice	
Tactical development	Emphasis on defence	Concede less than 10 points Direct ball to forwards	Develop tactical options	
Mental fitness	Commitment – goal-setting	Confidence – examine beliefs – positive self-talk	Control – calming techniques	Appropriate reading

MENTAL TRAINING STRATEGIES

A summary of the mental training strategies outlined throughout the book is presented here. When you identify a mental factor that you want to work on, select the appropriate strategy or combination of strategies. A short explanation of the technique may be required. This can be done at the start or finish of a training session. The technique can be incorporated into the next session and refined over a number of weeks like any new skill. When you feel competent try this technique out in a minor competition.

The strategies associated with each of the components of mental fitness are not exclusive to that component. Many of the strategies improve a number of aspects of mental fitness. Goal-setting helps strengthen commitment but as goals are achieved confidence grows. Setting short-term goals for training or competition helps improve concentration by focusing attention to specific cues.

STRATEGIES TO DEVELOP COMMITMENT	STRATEGIES TO BUILD CONFIDENCE
General goals **Performance profile** **Force field analysis** **Goal-setting**	**Examine beliefs** **Positive self-talk** **Thought stopping** **Reframing** **Affirmations**
STRATEGIES TO MAINTAIN CONTROL	STRATEGIES TO IMPROVE CONCENTRATION

Thought control techniques
(see under confidence)
Emotional control
  - calming techniques
  - simulated training
Imagery control
  - Relaxation
  - Imagining success
	Specific goal-setting
	Routines
	  - Pre-competition
	  - Competition-plan
	Trigger words
	Reminders
	Simulation training
	Distraction training

This book has highlighted the basic elements of mental fitness – commitment, confidence, control, concentration – and included a number of strategies to develop each of them. Other elements come under the scope of mental fitness but haven't been included here. If you are interested in any of these areas, there are many excellent resources covering such topics in detail. Topics that are relevant include:

Team-building

Leadership

Communication

Personality

Psychological reactions to injury

Mental training in injury rehabilitation

Burnout

Eating disorders

Retirement from sport

Children and sport

Just as there are more elements of mental fitness there are also other strategies that have not been featured in the book. When you get familiar with the strategies presented in this book and you are eager to develop further, seek out information on these strategies through reading, attending courses or workshops, and talking to experienced sportspeople, coaches, and relevant professionals such as sports educators or psychologists.

Appendix 1 and 2 lists some resources that will guide you further. Above all else you will become mentally stronger through action. Incorporate as many of the ideas presented in this book as often as you can, safe in the knowledge that winners are doing the same. Failure and setbacks will be part of your journey, but overleaf are some final words to remind you that success is never far away when you are giving it your best shot.

Don't quit

When things go wrong as they sometimes will,
When the road you're trudging seems all uphill,
When the funds are low and the debts are high,
And you want to smile, but you have to sigh,
When care is pressing you down a bit,
Rest if you must, but don't you quit.

Success is failure turned inside out,
The silver tint of the clouds of doubt,
And you never can tell how close you are,
It may be near when it seems afar,
So, stick to the fight when you're hardest hit,
It's when things go wrong that you must not quit.

Life is queer with its twists and turns,
As every one of us sometimes learns,
And many a person turns about
When they might have won had they stuck it out.
Don't give up though the pace seems slow -
You may succeed with another blow.

Often the struggler has given up
When he might have captured the victor's cup;
And he learned too late when the night came down,
How close he was to the golden crown.

APPENDIX 1

The books in the general section are biographies or collections of insights from well-known sports personalities. Like many other books of their type, they are helpful in that they describe the influences of mental factors in the lives of people from a range of sports. The books in the specific section analyse mental fitness and mental training in more depth.

General bibliography:

Anderson P: *Great Quotes from Great Sports Heroes*. USA: Career Press, 1997.

Bannister R: *The First Four Minutes*. London: The Sportsman's Book Club, 1956.

Corry E: *Kingdom Come*. Dublin, Ireland: Poolbeg Press, 1989.

Feinstein J: A *Good Walk Spoiled: Days and Nights on the PGA Tour*. London: Warner Books, 1996.

Ferguson HE: *The Edge: a guide to fulfiling dreams, maximising success and enjoying a lifetime of achievement*. Cleveland, Ohio, USA: Getting the Edge Company, 1983.

Hayes L, Hogan V, Walsh D: *Heroes of Irish Sporting Life*. Dublin: Multimedia, 1995

Johnson M: *Slaying the Dragon*. London: Piatkus, 1996.

Jones C: *What makes Winners win*. USA: Birch Lane Press, 1997

Longmore A: *Moments of Greatness, Touches of Class*. London: Kingswood Press, 1991.

Miller D, Coe S: *Running Free*. London: Sidgewick and Jackson, 1981.

Scally J: *100 Great Sporting Moments*. Dublin, Ireland: Blackwater Press, 1996.

Walton G: *Beyond Winning*. Champaign, Illinois, USA: Leisure Press, 1992.

Opposite: The agony of defeat – 1997 All-Ireland Club Hurling Final

Specific bibliography:

Bull SJ: *Sport Psychology: a self-help guide.* Marlborough, England: Crowood Press, 1991.

Butler G, Hope T: *Manage your Mind.* New York: Oxford University Press, 1995.

Loehr JE: *Mental Toughness Training for Sports: achieving athletic excellence.* Lexington, Massachusetts, USA: Stephen Green Press, 1982.

Martens R: *Coaches' Guide to Sport Psychology.* Champaign, Illinois, USA: Human Kinetics Publishers, 1997.

Moran A: *The Psychology of Concentration in Sports Performers.* England: Psychology Press,1996.

Nideffer RM: *Athletes' Guide to Mental Training.* Champaign, Illinois, USA: Human Kinetics Publishers, 1985.

Orlick T: *In Pursuit of Excellence: how to win in sport and life through mental training.* Champaign, Illinois, USA: Leisure Press, 1980.

Orlick T: *Coaches Training Manual to Psyching for Sport.* Champaign, Illinois, USA: Leisure Press, 1986.

Porter K, Foster J: *Visual Athletics.* USA: Wm C Brown Publishers, 1990

Sellars C: *Mental Skills: an introduction for sports coaches.* Leeds, England: The National Coaching Foundation, 1996.

Syer J, Connolly C: *Think to Win.* London, England: Simon & Schuster, 1991.

Vernacchia R, McGuire R, Cook D: *Coaching Mental Excellence.* USA : Warde Publishers, 1996.

Weinberg RS: *The Mental Advantage: developing your psychological skills in tennis.* Champaign, Illinois, USA: Leisure Press, 1988.

Waitley D: *The New Dynamics of Winning.* London: Nicholas Brealey Publishing, 1994.

APPENDIX 2

There are numerous audio cassettes available which provide useful guidelines on many of the mental training strategies outlined throughout the book. Most of them are available directly from the publishers.

Learn to Concentrate: Kate Smith and Dr. Aidan Moran
Learn to Relax: Kate Smith and Norman Brook
The Pressure Putt: Dr. Aidan Moran
These are available from: Tutorial Services (UK)
                            Freepost Bel 2575
                            Crumlin
                            Co. Antrim
                            BT 29 4BR
                            Northern Ireland

Inner Sports - Mental Skills for Peak Performance: Lydia Levleva
In Pursuit of Excellence: Terry Orlick
These are available from: Human Kinetics Europe
                            PO Box IW 14
                            Leeds
                            LS16 6TR
                            England

Performance Profiling: Richard Butler
Successful Coaching: Rainer Martens
These are available from: Coachwise Ltd.
                            Units 2/3 Chelsea Close
                            Off Amberly Road
                            Armley
                            Leeds
                            LS12 4HW
                            England

Useful addresses:

These addresses are good sources of more information. The publishers produce lists of their books and tapes, which you can order directly or from your bookshop. The coaching bodies produce literature audio tapes and videos which are useful to coaches and competitors. The National Coaching and Training Centre, Limerick, and the British National Coaching Foundation are very much involved in coach education and can supply information on courses. For information on specific coaching courses you can contact the relevant National Governing Body.

Publishers	Coaching bodies
Human Kinetics Europe,	National Coaching and Training Centre,
PO Box IW 14,	University of Limerick,
Leeds LS16 6TR,	Limerick,
England.	Ireland.
Coachwise Ltd,	National Coaching Foundation,
Units 2/3 Chelsea Close,	114 Cardigan Rd,
Off Amberly Road,	Headingley,
Armley,	Leeds LS6 3BJ,
Leeds LS12 4HW.	England.

Author Brendan Hackett can be contacted directly at:

Hazelhatch Road
Newcastle
Co. Dublin
Ireland
Tel / Fax: 01 458 8179
Email: bhackett@iol.ie

The Race

by D.H. Groberg

"Quit! Give up! You're beaten"
They shout at me and plead.
"There's just too much against you now.
This time you can't succeed!"

And as I start to hang my head
In front of failure's face
My downward fall is broken by
The memory of a race.

And hope refills my weakened will
As I recall that scene
For just the thought of that short race
Rejuvenates my being.

A children's race; young boys, young men
How I remember well.
Excitement, sure! but also fear
It wasn't hard to tell.

They all lined up so full of hope
Each thought to win that race.
Or tie for first, or if not that,
At least take second place.

And fathers watched from off the side
Each cheering for his son
And each boy hoped to show his dad
That he would be the one.

The whistle blew and off they went
Young hearts and hopes afire
To win and be the hero there
Was each young boy's desire.

And one boy in particular
Whose dad was in the crowd
Was running near the lead and thought:
"My dad will be so proud"

But as they speeded down the field
Across a shallow dip
The little boy who thought to win
Lost his step and slipped.

Trying hard to catch himself
His hand flew out to brace
And mid the laughter of the crowd
He fell flat on his face.

So down he fell and with him hope
He couldn't win it now
Embarrassed, sad he only wished
To disappear somehow.

But as he fell his dad stood up
And showed his anxious face
Which to the boy so clearly said
"Get up and win the race."

He quickly rose, no damage done
Behind a bit, that's all
And ran with all his mind and might
To make up for the fall

So anxious to restore himself
To catchup and to win
His mind went faster than his legs:
He slipped and fell again!

He wished then he had quit before
With only one disgrace
"I'm hopeless as a runner, now;
I shouldn't try to race."

But in the laughing crowd he searched
And found his father's face
That steady look which said again:
"Get up and win that race!"

So up he jumped to try again
Ten yards behind the last
"If I'm to gain those yards," he thought
"I've got to move real fast."

Exerting everything he had
He regained eight or ten
But trying so hard to catch the lead
He slipped and fell again!

Defeat. He lay there silently
A tear dropped from his eye
"There's no sense running anymore,
Three strikes; I'm out; Why try?"

The will to rise had disappeared
All hope had fled away
So far behind; so error prone
A loser all the way.

"I've lost, so what's the use," he thought
"I'll live with my disgrace."
But then he thought about his dad
Who soon he'd have to face.

"Get up," an echo sounded low,
"Get up and take your place;
You were not meant for failure here.
Get up and win the race."

"With borrowed will get up," it said,
"You haven't lost at all,
For winning is no more than this
To rise each time you fall."

So up he rose to run once more
And with a new commit
He resolved that win or lose
At least he wouldn't quit

So far behind the others now,
The most he'd ever been
Still he gave it all he had
And ran as though to win.

Three times he'd fallen, stumbling,
Three times he rose again
Too far behind to hope to win
He still ran to the end.

They cheered the winning runner
As he crossed the line first place
Head high, and proud, and happy
No falling; no disgrace.

But when the fallen youngster
Crossed the line last place
The crowd gave him the greatest cheer
For finishing the race.

And even though he came in last
With head bowed low, unproud,
You would have thought he won the race
To listen to the crowd

And to his dad he sadly said
"I didn't do so well."
"To me, you won" his father said
"You rose each time you fell."

And now when things seem dark
And difficult to face
The memory of that little boy
Helps me in my race.

For all of life is like that race
With ups and downs and all
And all you have to do is win
And rise each time you fall.

"Quit! Give up! You're beaten!"
They still shout in my face.
But another voice within me says:
"Get up and win that race!"